ROMANCE
with
ROMANS

ROMANCE

with

ROMANS

TED E. HURLBURT

Pleasant Word
A Division of WinePress Group
PW

Pleasant Word (a division of WinePress Publishing, PO Box 428, Enumclaw, WA 98022) functions only as book publisher. As such, the ultimate design, content, editorial accuracy, and views expressed or implied in this work are those of the author.

Unless otherwise noted, all Scriptures are taken from the *New American Standard Bible*, © 1960, 1963, 1968, 1971, 1972, 1973, 1975, 1977, 1995 by The Lockman Foundation. Used by permission.

ISBN 13: 978-1-4141-1547-4
ISBN 10: 1-4141-1547-4
Library of Congress Catalog Card Number: 2009907392

To the readers of this book: that you may be enriched in your faith and love of God, which will assure you of a lasting relationship with Him.

To receive the greatest blessing from this book, I suggest the following steps be taken while reading the book:

1. Open your Bible to the passage being studied.

2. Read the verses three times. The first time to see what it says and the second time to look for a key verse, one that just speaks to your heart. The third time is to allow His Word to soak into your heart and fill it with His truths.

3. Now you are ready to look into the content of *Romance with Romans*; you are ready to receive the most that this book has to offer. God will bless you.

Mr. Ted

CONTENTS

ACKNOWLEDGEMENTS

MY FIRST ACKNOWLEDGEMENT must be to God, who laid upon my heart to enter into this wonderful and blessed task. I owe Him my heartfelt thanks.

My profound thanks and gratitude is to the many who have aided in seeing that this book was written and printed:

To Dorothy, my wife, who has been and is the best friend, most honest critic, and greatest supporter I could ever dream of having.

To Leanna Pemberton, my daughter and missionary to Zimbabwe, who spent hours taking lectures from audiotapes that we made and typing them into a manuscript.

To Dr. Robert Reeves, who encouraged me to write this book and was very instrumental in seeing that the written page was correct and understandable as we modified, sometimes at great length, the spoken message that was on the tapes. Dr. Reeves is the author of *What Every Rookie Superintendent Should Know.*

To my niece, Gayle Niemeier, for proofreading, making suggestions, and raising questions that made some of the passages much more readable.

To Reba Harrison, for reading the manuscript and making valuable suggestions—I give you my thanks.

To Sherri Bigbee, who gave us direction in preparing the book for publishing and insight as to finding a publisher. She is the author of the novel *Lake of Spies.*

And, in conclusion, to all of the students who were so faithful in attending the class "Romance with Romans." Their questions and insights added much to this book.

INTRODUCTION

AS I HAVE taught and preached over the years, I have found that down-to-earth, easy-to-read, and understandable studies of the Bible intended for use by individuals and study groups are hard to come by. This observation has inspired me to develop an approach that will fill this void. In addition, I believe there is a great need for a commentary that weds two vital factors in a romance. These are: knowledge about the object of our adoration and feeling for the object of our adoration. Maybe I should explain further. The exposing of God's revealed Word to us by others ought to be aimed at stimulating our ears (knowledge) and stirring our hearts (feelings). The aim of this book is to provide for both these segments of our being, and hence, to enhance our love for God's Word. If we just play to the intellect and do not touch the emotions, we have missed the depth of the greatest love story ever written.

I wish very much for the readers of this book to have a better understanding of its content and to have a real love affair with the book of Romans. That is why the book is titled *Romance with Romans*. The approach that I have taken is set in this direction: Both the intellect and the emotions should be married together in our pursuit for truth as it is found in God's Word. As an example of this approach, let's consider the author of the book of Romans, Paul of Tarsus.

First, let's show an intellectual approach. Paul was born in Tarsus, which is located in the southwest corner of Turkey. After being schooled and trained at the feet of Gamaliel, one of the noted scholars of the Jewish Law, he became a Pharisee of Pharisees, extremely zealous for the preservation of the old covenant described in the Old Testament. However, after his confrontation with the Lord on the way to Damascus, he became a Christian and an evangelist.

Paul wrote Romans around 57 AD, on his third missionary journey, while at Corinth. Although he didn't fully realize it at the time, he was on his way back to Jerusalem to be jailed for two years before setting out for Rome under much different circumstances than could probably be imagined.

While all of that is well and good and true, often the hearer will say, "So what? How can a layman better understand what Paul was writing about?" In the pages of this book I will attempt to respond to this intellectual "so what."

Second, let's look at an example of the emotional approach. Paul was a man chosen by God to be an Apostle to the Gentiles. He uniquely fit the qualifications needed to become the great evangelist he was. He was born among the Gentiles and had his early rearing (probably up to the age of 12) influenced by the Gentile's thinking and culture. At that age he would have gone to Jerusalem for his Bar Mitzvah. For his further training, sometime later, he was either sent to, or his family moved to, Jerusalem, where he became thoroughly and fully indoctrinated with the Jewish Law. His brilliance led him to become a Pharisee of Pharisees, highly motivated to protect the Law of God at all costs.

When Christianity came in with the force of the Holy Spirit so that thousands and thousands (well over five thousand men) became Christians, Paul became their avowed enemy. Seeking the destruction of this "new cult," as the conservative traditionalist Jews called it, he asked for and got permission from the leadership to persecute those in it. After that, Paul journeyed afar, even to Damascus in Syria, to stamp out this perceived threat of this enemy to God's Law.

It was on his way to Damascus that God touched this man's life and heart—a man whom God knew understood the Gentile culture and who deeply appreciated that perfect Law that God had handed down to the Jews centuries earlier. God knew of his zeal, his marvelous way of communicating, and his heart's sensitivity. Paul was the one man who would go time and time again, missionary journey after missionary journey, to the Gentiles, a people whose lifestyle and thinking he knew and understood. Yet his devotion and compassion for the Jewish people never slackened. Paul was motivated by love, a love that drove him through stormy seas and hostile environments—suffering human abuse and being ridiculed and rejected by his own people. Yet Paul's love was so great that he would have tasted their hell, if it meant they would receive his heaven (Rom. 9:3).

Paul's love is poured out in the book of Romans. While we look at and view this letter—as great a doctrinal thesis as it is—remember that we will miss the great power of the book if we do not see the romance that Paul had with God and people.

Now we are ready to journey into a *Romance with Romans*. In our journey, we will observe that God's love for both the Gentiles and the Jews was exhibited and poured out by this one man. We will see both Paul's intellect and feelings playing out in this romance. They are poured out because of the wisdom of a great, powerful, and understanding God. In a like manner, I have taken in hand to create a commentary approach that shows both of these ideals, that is, his intellect and emotion.

INTRODUCTION

This book has been divided into sixteen chapters, which generally follow the chapters of Romans. Throughout, the New American Standard Bible is used. Study guide questions have been provided throughout and at the end of each chapter. The Bible and self-reflection provide the answers.

It is my prayer that as you read through *Romance with Romans* you will find in the epistle of Romans a deep love and appreciation for the message that this man, Paul, sent by God, has written to us.

THE GOSPEL—THE THEME
ROMANS 1:1–17

WE ARE GOING to have a Romance with Romans because we are going to fall in love with this book. We will fall in love with the message and the theme of this book and fall in love with the logical, orderly way in which Paul teaches.

By way of introduction, there are points of importance. From a logical standpoint, this book is one of the most fascinating books in the New Testament. It is a book in which Paul will ask a question and then, step-by-step, demonstrate how the answer to that question is derived. As a question is answered, it leads to another question, then another; and this is what makes this book so tremendously interesting. This is a pure "Paul style" of writing.

Remember that while the writers of the Bible were given the liberty to utilize their own style by God, they were nonetheless inspired in what they wrote. So there is really but one author of the sixty-six books of the Bible, and that is God. Still, each of about forty-four different writers of the Bible has his own particular, unique way of conveying the message of truth that God inspired.

As Paul writes in his unique style, we will see the attention he gives to two main cultures—the culture of the Roman Empire and the culture of the Jewish religion. The culture of the Roman Empire was centered on its imperialistic nature and dominating conquests of areas that today are Western Europe, all of the Balkan countries, all of the mid-east, and Northern Africa (as far south as Ethiopia and perhaps further). This vast conquest brought great wealth to the Empire, a sense of superiority, and a highly-inflated ego that led to the view that the need for any outside source for assistance or advice was unthinkable.

The Jewish culture was of a religious nature. The Jewish people felt that they were the chosen of God, protected and provided for by Him, and hence, superior to the entire

Gentile world—even with the Roman supremacy. In this line of thinking, they preached one message; but in their highly-inflated ego, they practiced a lifestyle foreign to the message. The thought of anyone other than a Jew being included in the family of God was unthinkable to them.

As the book of Romans focuses on these two cultures, it beautifully, sometimes tenderly, sometimes with tough love, points out the absolute need of each culture to be kissed by the grace of God, which is achievable only through faith in Jesus Christ.

Introduction to the Letter

Generally speaking, we should start at the very first verse of a book. But being the non-conformist that I am, I want to start with the sixteenth and seventeenth verses of the first chapter. Verse 16 says, "For I am not ashamed of the gospel, for it is the power of God for salvation to everyone who believes, to the Jew first and also to the Greek." Verse 17 states, "For in it the righteousness of God is revealed from faith to faith; as it is written, *but the righteous man shall live by faith.*"

These two verses state the theme of the book. Everything within the book, or at least within the first eleven chapters of the book, relates back to the theme. The theme is: the Gospel has power. The power of the Gospel leads to salvation for everyone who believes. The faith factor comes in, to the Jew first and also to the Greek (or the Gentile, the non-Jew), and it reveals the righteousness of God from faith unto faith. (Faith unto faith has reference to the faith of those who lived under the Old Covenant as well as to the faith of those who live under grace or the New Covenant. See Romans 3:25 and Hebrews 11.)

The Gospel must be articulated and understood so that the power that leads us to salvation leads us to a place where, through the Holy Spirit, human reason, and stable faith, we can accept the truths that are within the Gospel. Here, within this power, we find a relationship with God regardless of our supposed secular or religious superiority. As expressed in Romans 10:11–15: "For the Scripture says, *whoever believes in him will not be disappointed.* For there is no distinction between Jew and Greek; for the same Lord is Lord of all, abounding in riches for all who call upon Him; for *whoever will call on the name of the lord will be saved.* How then will they call upon Him in whom they have not believed? And how shall they believe in Him whom they have not heard? And how shall they hear without a preacher? And how shall they preach unless they are sent? Just as it is written, *how beautiful are the feet of those who bring glad tidings of good things!*"

Introduction of Paul and the Gospel

Romans 1:1–2

Now, let's return to Romans 1:1, which says, "Paul, a bond-servant of Christ Jesus, called as an apostle, set apart for the gospel of God…" There should be no question as to who is the writer of the book. This specifically states that Paul is the writer. Asking who wrote Romans would be about as intelligent as asking, "Who is buried in Grant's tomb?"

Paul starts by stating three positions that he holds. First he describes himself as being a "bond-servant of Christ." This is not the only time that he describes himself as being a bond-servant. The book of Philippians and the book of Titus begin by saying Paul is a bond-servant. Then the book of Philemon starts out by saying, "Paul, a prisoner of Christ." I like that. He has been captured, and he is captivated by the glory and the beauty of Christ. He didn't say "a prisoner of Rome," because he would not succumb to his being in prison as an inhibiting factor—he was a prisoner of Christ.

To better understand what a bond-servant was, we need to look at the different types of servant's in Paul's day. There were three forms of servitude in the Roman economy in the first century. First, there was a very trusted servant; he was so trusted that he was almost counted as a part of the family. Because of the lack of rapid transportation and fast communication, people sent out these trusted servants with sometimes large amounts of goods or money to invest for them in other places. Their means of communication would just drive us wild today; we couldn't handle it. (We think our snail mail is slow compared to our e-mail.) One example of this type of servant is the story about Philemon and his servant Onesimus, who betrayed that trust. The second kind of servant was the domestic servant, who would do tasks such as gardening, being the nanny for the children, and doing the housework. The third type of servant was the bond-servant, the lowest form of a servant. That is literally what they were: They were shackled. They would work in the salt pits or work as oarsmen on the boats; and if the boats sank, they were shackled to them! The bond-servants felt the lashes of the task master. If they were not literally in chains they were branded as a slave (Ex. 21:6).

Paul places himself in the lowest category of servitude. He places himself in that position before he places himself in the position of an apostle. He does so because this is the position in which he viewed Christ when He offered Himself for us, as seen in Philippians 2: 7, "…but emptied Himself, taking the form of a bond-servant, and being made in the likeness of men." I think this attitude and posture of the apostle Paul is what made him great. God was able to work through his bond-servant, because Paul took that position. He ascribes to Jesus as being a bond-servant, even unto death, and that was the ultimate destiny of the bond-servant. He was lashed, shackled, and chained or nailed to the place of his death. It was Paul's desire to spiritually emulate Christ's life in his life (Gal 2:20).

How many "men of the cloth" today do what Paul did? We all must have the letters (or degrees) behind our names and all the reverence and the most high and the most holy and the most something or other in front of our names on the church marquee. I have yet to see a church marquee that said the name of the preacher was "bond-servant."

The second position of Paul was that he was "called to be an apostle." The closest thing that we have to an apostle in the secular world today would be an ambassador to a country. There was more than one apostle, but there is usually just one ambassador to each nation. That person may have a lot of underlings, but there is only one who is sent to be the spokesperson for the government to the government that has been recognized. The apostles were not representing a country, however; they were the ambassadors of God. They were the ones who were sent to represent the great kingdom of God and of Christ Jesus. So Paul was called to be sent, and then he was set apart. He was set apart for the Gospel of God. He was set apart to articulate the "glad tidings" or "Good News of God." We could follow no greater example than Paul's in being an articulator of that Good News.

The third position that Paul occupied was being "set apart for the Gospel of God." His life was to be spent in articulating that Good News of salvation to the Gentile world. If he had to use his skills as a tent maker, it was only to earn money so he could continue to preach. The setting apart to the Gospel was not a vocation, a profession, or an occupation; it was an obsession. Paul was ordained by God, was set apart for the Gospel, and was God's ambassador to the Gentiles. Paul was compelled by a servitude that was so binding that he chose to articulate the Gospel above his own personal welfare. His being set apart for the Gospel cost him much suffering—he was stoned, whipped, imprisoned, and, ultimately, paid the supreme price of having his life taken because of his articulation of the message of God. (Parenthetically, may I add, we need more pastors and ministers cut from the same cloth as Paul.)

Let's continue with Romans 1:2, which states, "…which He promised beforehand through His prophets in the holy Scriptures…" This Good News Paul is sharing is the long-promised message of inclusion and redemption. Of what did the "glad tidings" or "Good News" consist? In verses three and four, we find what is articulated or defined as the Gospel. The Gospel was promised beforehand through God's prophets in the Holy Scriptures so that the promise of Good News did not come at the event of Jesus' ministry. It was a promised Gospel that began at the birth of Jesus. There is a Gospel message in the Old Testament, and that Gospel message consists of all the messianic prophecies regarding the coming of Jesus Christ, who is the Good News. It hadn't arrived then, but in Bethlehem it did, just as it was promised beforehand by God (Matt. 2: 5–6). These scriptures, then, are the messianic scriptures, or those of the coming Messiah. That word "messianic" may sound bad (messy), but it is a good word. It has reference to the Messiah and means "according to or concerning God's Son."

8

QUESTIONS AND DISCUSSION FOR THE INTRODUCTION OF PAUL AND THE GOSPEL

1. Memorize Romans 1:16–17.

2. Name the two cultures that Romans addresses and tell about them.

3. How did Paul identify himself? (See verse 1.)

4. What three levels of servitude were there when Paul wrote Romans?

5. How do you personally feel about being a bond-servant to Christ?

6. Is there a difference between the author and writer of Romans? Who is the author, and who is the writer?

7. How does the theme of the book describe the Gospel? (See verses 16–17.)

8. How does this information apply to your life?

Introduction of Jesus, the Good News of God

Romans 1: 3–7

The way God identifies His Son to the Romans is shrewd—it really is! He states here in Romans 1:3, "…concerning His Son, who was born of a descendant of David according to the flesh…" This is saying that Christ had in Him royal blood. From an earthly or fleshly standpoint, He could hob-knob with the kings and the rulers of the world. Isn't it fascinating the way Paul kind of slips that in there? He just points out to the Church of Rome that they need not be intimidated by the power of Caesar. They were, and we as believers today are, following One of royalty. Fascinating! And that is Good News; it especially was to those who were in Rome.

Romans 1:4 goes on to say, "…who was declared with power to be the Son of God by the resurrection from the dead, according to the Spirit of holiness, Jesus Christ our Lord…" Jesus was born of a woman, born of the flesh, and was declared with power. How was Jesus in His ministry declared with power? There were two ways. First, He was declared with power by His teaching. Mark 1:22 states, "They were amazed at His teaching; for He was teaching them as one having authority, and not as the scribes." Jesus preaches to us, not as one who is parroting or repeating others, but rather as one who is initiating what He taught. All of our teaching and all of our preaching really is parroting, isn't it? In other words, we are reciting that which has been handed down to us; thus all of our teaching is parroting. Those in prior times also were simply articulating what others had taught, but not so with Jesus. His teaching was with authority, as though it had been initiated by Him. This is what makes the teachings of Jesus so absolutely phenomenal. This is what gives Him the breath of freshness. This is that which lifts Him above other teachers; He is the initiator of truth, and in His teachings He articulated that which He Himself initiated.

The second way Jesus was declared with power was through His works. The miracles that He performed demonstrated the power that was His. This is so beautifully seen in John 2:11: "This beginning of His signs Jesus did in Cana of Galilee, and manifested His glory, and His disciples believed in Him." This was in the wake of the first miracle that Jesus performed. It set the pattern for other miracles. His doing miracles that displayed His power does not mean that Jesus was lacking compassion when He performed miracles. He was (and is) indeed a compassionate God. Jesus had compassion for the blind, for the deaf, for the sick, and for those who had suffered great loss through death. He had great compassion for those who were taken in the very act of sexual immorality. He had compassion for those who had lived a sordid life. He had compassion for the crooked politician. But the miracles that He performed were not only motivated by this compassion, but also demonstrated His authority over sickness, nature, death, and demons. His miracles gave credence to and confirmed the truths He was teaching. We see His miracles and teachings working hand in hand.

There was no activity that Satan could produce that could overwhelm the power of Jesus. John points this out. John 1:5 says, "The Light shines in the darkness; and the darkness did not comprehend it." If the world could have overcome the power of Jesus, we wouldn't be here. But Jesus' power prevails, in spite of walls, in spite of dictators, and in spite of those in false religions who kill Christians (and even themselves) because they are not of the same order. Amazing! Jesus' power prevails over all. There is no power that can withstand the Spirit of Holiness. This is the power, the great power in the Son of God, and this power is dynamically manifested in all of Jesus' miracles. Jesus also dynamically manifested this power upon the cross. Then the most dynamic manifestation is seen in the emptiness of the tomb. Of course, there could not have been a resurrection that meant so much had there not been the passion of Christ that led Him to the cross to be sin for us (2 Cor. 5:21).

As we saw before, Romans 1:4 says, "...according to the Spirit of holiness...." Let's look at this from a grammatical standpoint. You have a prepositional phrase "of holiness." A prepositional phrase goes back and modifies or clarifies its antecedent, which in this case would be "the Spirit." The prepositional phrase can also be a possessive phrase, and this is one of possession. In other words, "the Spirit" that possesses holiness is the "Spirit of holiness." Initially, the term "holy" was used as an adjective that donates or speaks in regard to the character of the subject. "The spirit" being the subject, "holiness," then, was a description of the subject. Later, because it was so unique, for there is only One who is holy, the term "holy" no longer was an adjective, but a part of a proper noun, which denotes the name "Holy Spirit." So these two terms can be used interchangeably, whether it is "the spirit of holiness," which denotes possession, or the "Holy Spirit," which denotes character as well as possession.

Paul goes on to talk about the benefits of the Gospel in Romans 1:5: "through whom we have received grace and apostleship to bring about the obedience of faith among all the Gentiles for His name's sake." The benefits of Jesus being born of the flesh, the benefits of that power, the benefits of the resurrection, the benefits of that spirit of holiness cause in us a desire to be obedient. As Paul talks about those benefits, the first thing that he brings out is "through whom we have received grace." There isn't one of us who deserves what God has given, but neither is there one of us who cannot receive what God has given. That's the beauty of grace, the unmerited gift of forgiveness from God. That sums up in a capsule, and probably in an over simplistic manner, the beautiful nature of grace. We will see that concept really develop as we get into the fifth, sixth, and seventh chapters of Romans.

Consider the phrase in verse 5: "…through whom we have received…" Paul is speaking here using the term "we," so much, that I'm going to offer an opinion: Paul's relationship with the Lord was so great that he felt as though it was no longer "I" but "we." Paul uses the term "we" more often than he uses the term "I."

Verse 5 says, "…through whom we have received grace and apostleship to bring about the obedience of faith…" First of all, we have indicated the action of God, undeserved by man yet available to man—grace. Then we find the response to that action—an "obedience of faith." Faith is not just a mental belief in deity, nor is it just belief in the deity of Jesus or the articulating of that through a prayer. Faith has responsibility—"obedience" through faith. We are going to see this later, in the third and forth chapters, where there is a work of faith. This is not to be misunderstood as a work apart from faith. The works apart from faith cannot save; also faith apart from works cannot save (James 2:17). So how do we correspond and relate with faith and works? That will be fully discovered as we go through this book of Romans.

See how this introduction is so full of the gems that we are going to be digging up as we delve deeper into our romance with Romans? Take the gem in Romans 1:5: "…the obedience of faith among all Gentiles, for His name's sake…" Oh, I am so glad that is there, because that's like my name and your name are written here in the Scriptures (since I am a Gentile). This verse is a reemphasizing of Acts 2:39. A demonstration of this is Paul's ministry to the Gentiles over the previous years, including all three missionary journeys and one later back to Jerusalem.

Romans 1:6 continues, "…among whom you also are the called of Jesus Christ…" Consider the grammar in this verse. You can turn it around the other way and say Christ Jesus, the Messiah Jesus. The term "Christ" was an adjective used to describe Jesus. But "Christ" was so commonly used with the name Jesus that it became a part of His name. Hence, both are capitalized.

11

As we move to Romans 1:7, it says, "…to all who are beloved of God in Rome, called as saints: Grace to you and peace from God our Father and the Lord Jesus Christ." Paul is writing this to those recipients in Rome who had received grace, and oh, if there was ever a city that didn't deserve it, it was Rome. There would only be one that deserved it even less, and that was Jerusalem. Yet here, they are called the beloved of God through their obedience to faith. In spite of great oppression, they exercised that obedience and committed their lives to the lordship of Jesus. Let's continue in verse 7, "…Grace to you and peace from God our Father and the Lord Jesus Christ." We see another adjective or proper name that is associated with Jesus. Sometimes we drop that first name (Lord) and think of Jesus Christ as our Savior. We need to come to grips with His being the Lord of our lives, with our being bond-servants in chains to His will. That is really getting to know God.

QUESTIONS AND DISCUSSION FOR INTRODUCTION OF JESUS, THE GOOD NEWS OF GOD

1. Name the two ways in which Jesus demonstrated His Power. (See verses 3–4.)

2. What part of speech was "holy" when used with "Spirit" before, and why is it now used differently? (See verse 4.)

3. Grace is the result of what events? (See verses 4–5.)

4. How can this information apply to your life?

Giving Thanks To God

Romans 1:8–17

In Romans 1:8–15 we find that there are a number of thanks to God. We see thanks made to God for the recipients of the letter, beloved ones in God's eyes, and thanks made to God for Paul, himself, and more so for the ministry that he had, denoting his desire to share this good news with them. Let's quickly go over these thanks.

First of all, Paul wants to thank God for the recipients of the letter (Romans 1:8–10). Verse 8 says, "First, I thank my God through Jesus Christ for you all because your faith is being proclaimed throughout the whole world." Do we ever take time out to run down the church roster and bring each member there before the throne of grace and say, "God I thank you for that person"? They may not be all that I expect them to be, but then I'm probably not all that they expect me to be. I can just thank God for them. I can find some qualities in their lives for which I can thank God. If we as a church would do that type of thing more often, there certainly would be a lot fewer criticisms within congregations regarding one another. We don't know the journey people have taken, the steps they have had to climb, the cross they have had to bear, or the progress they have made. It may to us seem minuscule, but to them it is monumental, and we need to thank God for everyone who walks with Jesus.

If I could make an assignment for you, it would be this: Go home, take your church membership book, and before the sun sets again, spend some time going down through every name. Even though you may not know them, just thank God for them, and ask God to be close to them. Pray that God will help them carry whatever burden they have this day. Tell God that you love them. What a bond of great Christian love and faith there is and would be in all of the congregations if this were done. Paul just thanks God for every one of them. What a way to open a letter!

Verses 9 and 10 say, "For God, whom I serve in my spirit in the preaching of the gospel of His Son, is my witness as to how unceasingly I make mention of you, always in my prayers making requests, if perhaps now at last by the will of God I may succeed in coming to you." Paul had tried many times to go to Rome, but he had always been diverted. Then there was the matter of funds. A trip to Rome was expensive. Well, Paul's prayer to go to Rome was soon to be answered in the most mysterious way. God heard Paul's prayer, heard the longing of his heart, and created a way in which Rome itself would pick up the tab for his voyage. That is the way God works. It might not be the way that we would have anticipated (it wasn't first class lounge berths). However, Paul turned out, though a prisoner, to be the captor's savior—not spiritually—but physically, and that is also the way God works. Physically Paul was a prisoner on a boat caught in a storm and doomed to destruction. When all seemed hopeless and lost, the very presence of Paul allowed them all to reach land safely (Acts 27:42–44).

Romans 1:11 says, "For I long to see you so that I may impart some spiritual gift to you, that you may be established…" We have done such an injustice to this verse by limiting it to the qualifications of a certain number of gifts that are mentioned (see 1 Cor. 12). All of us have a spiritual gift we can give to people. Everyone in some way has shared a spiritual gift. I have been buoyed and strengthened by the spiritual gifts people have imparted. Consider the non-believer—for example, a non-believing clerk in a grocery store. Sometimes clerks have a pretty hard time. They get some pretty nasty people in there. If we, as Christians, can just go in and have a smile and say a good word and ask them how they are doing, it means a lot. The next time we go through a checkout line, the clerks are going to remember us, because we imparted a type of spiritual gift to them. We buoyed them up in their hearts and in their distress. We helped to smooth the way. This is so easily done. When we see and greet one another, it can be done with warmth, compassion, and love for all. We are imparting a spiritual gift. It doesn't mean that we have to learn how to speak or how to play the piano or how to lead singing or how to sing solos or how to be good in youth work or anything else. All of those are spiritual gifts, and they do bless us. However, we can be the drabbest person on the totem pole as far as personality is concerned and still share a spiritual gift with another person. That should be our goal. God help us this day to share a spiritual gift—to show to others the radiance and peace of Christ that is in our lives.

Paul continues in Romans 1:12, "...that is, that I may be encouraged together with you while among you, each of us by the other's faith, both yours and mine." Now consider the results of sharing a spiritual gift. This establishes the receiver of that spiritual gift. When others see you and see you work through some of the struggles that you have had and see your courage, what does that do to them? It establishes their confidence in Christ. They are more rooted and grounded so that it is not only the person who gave the spiritual gift that is blessed but also the recipient of that spiritual gift. Verse 12 contains the phrase "encouraged together with you." That is the spiritual gift as I understand it. I would completely divorce the gifts mentioned in 1 Corinthians 12 from this verse. What Paul is talking about here, is each of us by faith—both yours and others'—imparting that gift of spirituality to one another. Isn't it great to belong to the family of God and to have the fellowship and warmth that is seen in a congregation?

Romans 1:13 says, "I do not want you to be unaware, brethren, that often I have planned to come to you (and have been prevented thus far) so that I may obtain some fruit among you also, even as among the rest of the Gentiles." Wow! Here is this apostle, this great articulator of the Gospel, an evangelist who overshadows Billy Sunday and Billy Graham and all of the rest of them, saying (my paraphrase), "I want to come to you because I want to share in your fruit. I want to be spiritually blessed by you." There is no room for arrogance in leadership!

Paul goes on to say in Romans 1:14, "I am under obligation both to Greeks and to barbarians, both to the wise and to the foolish." In other words, he is saying (again, my paraphrase), "My apostleship is not a vocation, an occupation, or a profession; it is an obsession. I am obligated." Oh, if that could be the hearts of the ministers today. It is disturbing to me that so many preachers are being turned out by so many of our theological schools whose first questions are about what the medical benefits and vacation benefits are and what the salary is going to be. They ask this before they ever ask about the spiritual dynamics—it is truly heartbreaking.

Let's move on to Romans 1:15–17. Verse 15 says, "So, for my part, I am eager to preach the gospel to you also who are in Rome." Paul gets to the theme in this verse. We know what the Gospel is, what it contains, and what affect the Good News has, both to the bearer and to the recipient. Thus, like Paul, I am not ashamed—no fear, no shame. I am not ashamed in Christ Jesus, who is the promise revealed in the prophecies. I am not ashamed in Christ Jesus, in the articulating of this Good News of the power of God unto salvation. As Paul says in verse 16, "For I am not ashamed of the gospel, for it is the power of God for salvation to everyone who believes, to the Jew first and also to the Greek." After the resurrection of Jesus, God gave

His people forty years to accept Him. Forty years is typically used in the Scriptures as a time of trial. He gave them forty years. Forty years almost to the day is when, in 73 A.D., Masada, the last fortress of Israel, fell. Three years before that, Jerusalem fell.

Verse 17 says, "For in it the righteousness of God is revealed from faith to faith; as it is written, '*but the righteous man shall live by faith.*'" Did God reveal this righteousness in the Law? Yes, He did. But in the Law the consequence is justice without mercy and there is very little, if any, grace. In Christ there is the revealing of the righteousness of God, not in a code written upon cold, dead stone by the blazing finger of God like in the Old Testament, but in Jesus, who came to earth in the flesh. Hang on to that bit of righteousness, because we are not going to lose sight of it as we delve into Romans. Grab hold of verse 17: "For in it the righteousness of God is revealed from faith to faith; as it is written, '*but the righteous man shall live by faith.*'"

In the next chapter we are going to show how needed, how absolutely needed, this Gospel message is. There is, never has been, and never will be, one person, regardless of background, who is not in need of this great Gospel. We have laid the groundwork, and now we are going to plow into the great need of the Roman Empire, with its supposed superiority, and the false Jewish concept that they would forever be the only children of God.

QUESTIONS AND DISCUSSION FOR GIVING THANKS TO GOD

1. Paul was thankful for whom? (See verse 8.)

2. What would be a blessed homework assignment?

3. Why was Paul eager to go to Rome? (See verse 11.)

4. What is revealed in the Gospel? (See verses 16–17.)

5. How can this information apply to your life?

ALL-INCLUSIVE NEED
ROMANS 1:18–3:20

Introduction

IN THIS CHAPTER we will see the all-inclusive need for Christ. There are none so wicked that they cannot come and none so righteous that they should not come.

Paul wanted to preach the Gospel. As we look at the Gospel itself, we find the declaration of the power of God unto salvation, and this power is to those who believe—to the Jew first and also to the Gentile. This Gospel is not the initial Good News of God nor is it the last Good News from God. It is the center of that Good News, which previous Good News was looking for and post Good News follows in the wake of the person of Jesus (note Rom. 3:25). Jesus' life, death, burial, and resurrection are the cause for the Good News of salvation, which reaches every generation until the consummation of time. The Good News is that, because of Jesus, at the consummation of time as we on earth know it, we can have that never-ending relationship with God, in His presence. The Good News of the Gospel, all of the Good News prior to the coming of Jesus, was looking forward to that coming. The Good News following the coming of Jesus is a result of the fact that He did come. Therefore, we conclude that the Gospel is the hub of all Good News regarding our relationship with God.

In a small church there is great power, but relative to a church 120 times its size, we might say it isn't much. Power of anything is relative. Consider a gasoline engine, a one-cylinder, two-stroke puttsy, puttsy. It has a certain amount of power, but it doesn't have anything compared to a Lincoln Continental. So, likewise, by what standard of measurement are we going to evaluate the power of God regarding salvation? Regardless of the system of measurement we contrive, once we see what the power overcomes, we can appreciate the thrust and the force of that power. Romans 1:18 through 3:18 is devoted to showing the power, the magnitude, and the universality of the Gospel to overcome the universal drag of sin. Its power will then lift the bedraggled sinner into a spiritual orbit to be included with the host of heaven.

The need for the Gospel and how deep and desperate that need is will become evident by the time we get to the middle of the third chapter. That is where we see the revealing of the righteousness of God. We can appreciate all the more the righteousness of God, which is sufficient to overcome the universality and depth of sin. So these next few verses are not going to be what you would call charming verses. They depict sin in its universality and in its awfulness. But remember, this is to show the power of the Gospel that is greater than the power of sin. We must comprehend how great sin is to appreciate the greatness of the Gospel's power.

Power to Overcome the Sins of the Gentiles

Romans 1:18–32

Romans 1:18 to the end of the chapter deals with the sin of those who are not Jews. This would initially deal with the readers, who are Romans, and other Gentiles.

Remember that the theme verses in this book are found in Romans 1:16–17. These state in part that the Gospel is the power of God unto salvation for everyone who believes, to the Jew first and also to the Greek. Why then does Paul start out by talking about those who are Romans? Wouldn't it have been more logical for him to start out with the Jews and then discuss the Gentiles? Yet Paul starts with the Romans. He is writing this letter to Gentiles; hence, he starts out with them. His writing depicts so clearly the falling, decay, and depravity of Rome that ultimately led to the demise of that great empire. Reading this, we may be able to see similarities to what is going on today in the United States, and we shudder, realizing that the fall of our great nation can take place not just from outside forces, but also from inside corruption. Inner corruption is our country's greatest enemy!

Romans 1:18 says, "For the wrath of God is revealed from heaven against all ungodliness and unrighteousness of men who suppress the truth in unrighteousness…" The emphasis is on the term "all." God's wrath is not ethnically, socially, materially, or educationally limited. You can't get away with murder with God because you were a great football player or a TV star or a politician. There is equality in the administrating of God's wrath, even as there is equality in the administrating of His grace. Sometimes people feel God will excuse them for unrighteousness because of their position or length of service or works or whatever attribute they use to rationalize their behavior. I have seen this with one of my dear preacher friends, a great articulator of the Scriptures. He spoke with just enough of an accent to enchant people. He felt, because of his position, his outward piety, and his oratorical ability, that God would excuse him from promiscuousness, but he was mistaken. God is against "all" unrighteousness. It doesn't matter how long we have served or how high we climb; unrighteousness is cause for a fall. It is the sinful deeds that are committed that suppress the truth. Unrighteousness will take the principles of truth, twist them around, and force them back against truth. When somebody is crying out so strongly that something is so, so wrong, over and over again, and he is obsessed with this, it is time, psychologically speaking, to take note, because maybe he is trying to get cleansed of his own sinful practice.

Paul continues in Romans 1:19–23. Verses 19 and 20 say, "…because that which is known about God is evident within them; for God made it evident to them. For since the creation of the world His invisible attributes, His eternal power and divine nature, have been clearly seen, being understood through what has been made, so that they are without excuse." The earth does display God's handiwork. People may not believe in God correctly because they have not been taught. But still there is that inherent and innate longing within the hearts of people to reach out beyond themselves. Even in the most barbaric societies there is some form of worship because they see Him in creation. Almost always in paganism there is worship of creation in some form—the sun, the stars, the moon, lighting, thunder, etc. They have no scientific explanation for it; it is beyond their control, so to them it must be a god.

It just follows in simple logic, as seen at the end of verse 20, "…so that they are without excuse." Natural law does not allow excuse! The violation of that natural law, whether it is external or internal, has consequences. The results of going against natural law can be seen in verses 21–22: "For even though they knew God, they did not honor Him as God or give thanks, but they became futile in their speculations, and their foolish heart was darkened. Professing to be wise, they became fools…" Who were the smartest, most learned men on earth back in the days before Christ? Wasn't the center of learning, great thought, and mathematics in Greece? Do not the greatest philosophers even now reference Homer, Socrates, etc? Yet they became foolish because they, as it states in verses 22–23, "…became fools, and exchanged the glory of the incorruptible God for an image in the form of corruptible man and of birds and four-footed animals and crawling creatures." They needed an object to worship. Because they couldn't see or understand God, they supplanted Him with an object to worship. We can see this behavior way back in the Israelites' exodus from Egypt. When Moses was up on the mountain, what did the people do? They took up a mandatory collection, not voluntary; they stripped everyone of their gold, and then they fashioned a golden calf. Even though the hand of an unseen God had led them through the Red Sea, brought them deliverance from slavery, and saved their firstborn from death, they worshipped a powerless golden calf of their own creation. And ultimately, three thousand of them died because of it.

Let's continue to Romans 1:24. "Therefore God gave them over in the lusts of their hearts to impurity, so that their bodies would be dishonored among them." Lust is just the opposite of love—but as we have said before, Satan can take and twist things around. Love is that which does not consider a reward for what it does. If there is any truth regarding the activity of love, it is found in 1 Corinthians 13. In that chapter we see that love is always giving, always giving, always giving. Lust, on the other hand, is always seeking self-gratification. What does the world call lust today? People call it "love." Can you see how this has completely debased their appreciation for what constitutes true love? God says He gave them over to their lusts—to self-gratification. "For they exchanged the truth of God for a lie, and worshiped and served the creature rather than the Creator, who is blessed forever. Amen" (Romans 1:25).

God gave them over to their passions. The greatest example of passion we have is seen in the Passion of Christ. What does His passion mean? It means His love—His purpose, that which motivated His living, His goal, His powerful aim. However, the passions of the Romans were to fulfill their lusts for domination, riches, and self-gratification. This is the power of sin within the world then and today, and it can only be eradicated through the power of the Gospel.

Romans 1:26–27 goes on to say, "For this reason God gave them over to degrading passions; for their women exchanged the natural function for that which is unnatural, and in the same way also the men abandoned the natural function of the woman and burned in their desire towards one another, men with men committing indecent acts and receiving in their own persons the due penalty of their error." Here we see the result of God giving them over to their passions. I don't know of anything that can be more descriptive of the acts of homosexuality and the results of those acts than what is expressed in those two verses. Notice there is a penalty due for their error. Through the media we are told that there is alarm among those in the medical field because of the dramatic increase of AIDS, especially in San Francisco—duh! It doesn't take a rocket scientist to figure that one out! However, those lost ones don't see anything wrong with their behavior, and they view those who do as bigots who are full of prejudice. Oh, the twists and turns that Satan performs are never changing.

Romans 1:28–31 says, "And just as they did not see fit to acknowledge God any longer, God gave them over to a depraved mind, to do those things which are not proper, being filled with all unrighteousness, wickedness, greed, evil; full of envy, murder, strife, deceit, malice; they are gossips, slanderers, haters of God, insolent, arrogant, boastful, inventors of evil, disobedient to parents, without understanding, untrustworthy, unloving, unmerciful…" Other than that, they were pretty nifty people! This is the power and the grip of sin upon the hearts of people. This is the power Jesus can and has overcome. If the power of this sin is greater than the power of the Gospel, then all would be hopeless, for we would be trapped in our depravity. However, there is the power that God has that can strip away all sin, no matter how deeply engrained within the society and within the hearts of people. He can do it! It may cause a number of towers to come down. It may cause a number of calamities to occur. It may cause the voice of the righteous to rise up in every election and defeat every immoral proposition that comes pouncing upon us, but God will overcome. His power is greater than evil.

Is this the most sinful generation that has ever lived? Every generation seems to be the most sinful to those living in that generation. Every generation since Jesus' crucifixion and resurrection also has had an availability of the power of the Gospel of Christ. When we read of the sordid history of Rome, even with all of the sin and degradation we have, our generation looks like a Sunday school picnic. Whole villages and whole nations were completely destroyed. Depravity was abundant. Not only was it men with men and women with women, but also it was people with beasts. I wouldn't be surprised if there was an endeavor in our society to legalize relations with beasts next!

To us, our generation may seem the worst, but it is also the best. It can be made better by the power of the Gospel. It will get worse by the power of sin. Hence, the mission of the church becomes all the more pertinent and important. In the church is where this passion for right needs to be greater than the world's passion for wrong.

Romans 1:32 says, "…and although they know the ordinance of God, that those who practice such things are worthy of death, they not only do the same, but also give hearty approval to those who practice them." It is passion that drives a person. If the passion is for evil, then the practice follows; and the practice of those evil deeds is so great that that person will continue in them and give approval to those who passionately practice them.

QUESTIONS AND DISCUSSION FOR
POWER TO OVERCOME THE SINS OF THE GENTILES

1. What truths does unrighteousness try to suppress? (See verses 18–20.)

2. Give reasons for these truths being invalid to an unbeliever. (See verse 21.)

3. The glory of God is exchanged for what and by whom? (See verse 23.)

4. Describe the depth of evil passion.

5. What are the results of homosexuality? (See verses 26–27.)

6. Is it the sinner or the sin that has to be dishonored?

7. Why is the theme of the book of Romans relevant to Gentiles?

8. Where do you fit into this picture?

Let's look at Romans 1:32 again: "And although they know the ordinance of God, that those who practice such things are worthy of death, they not only do the same, but also give hearty approval to those who practice them." This is what I refer to as a swing verse. It concludes the establishing of one application of principles to an object, the Gentiles. The application now will be applied to another object, the chosen people of God, the Jews. Up until Christ, they had held that exclusive position. We will now explore the desperate need of the Jews and then relate that in principle to "churchianity" as we see it today.

Power to Overcome the Sins of the Jews

Romans 2:1–2:29

In chapter two, Paul is going to start addressing the children of God.

Romans 2:1 begins, "Therefore you are without excuse, everyone of you who passes judgment, for in that which you judge another, you condemn yourself; for you who judge practice the same things." He will start out with the Christian; he will then bring the Jews in. Fasten your seat belts, and curl up your toes…because they are going to get stomped on. Remember, the power of the Gospel is greater than all sin! Keep that in the back of your mind.

Romans 2:2–3 continues, "And we know that the judgment of God rightly falls upon those who practice such things. But do you suppose this, O man, when you pass judgment on those who practice such things and do the same yourself, that you will escape the judgment of God?" Question—if we are driven by the passions of our body and by selfish motives, and if the passion of our mind is keyed on "what is in it for me," then what really is there? Aren't we all in the same boat?

I recently received a telephone call from a lady who said, "I have two kids, and I want to be at your church Sunday morning. Do you have something for the kids?"

I asked, "Well, how old are they?"

"One is 10 and the other is 12. Do you have a Junior Worship?"

"Well, not exactly. But we do have preparations by which we can accommodate them. We have a tremendous puppet program here, just tailor-made for that age."

"You don't have a regular Junior Worship?"

Well, I hated to say no, so I said, "Well, we can accommodate them."

She didn't show up. You see, she wanted to be served and yet was unwilling to serve. She could have said, "I will bring my two children and assist you in having a junior church program if you would like." But she lacked the passion to serve. She wanted her children and herself to be served, but she chose not to offer herself as a servant. So much of the "churchianity" population today is saying, "What can I get out of it?" Rather than, "What can I contribute to it?"

Romans 2:4: "Or do you think lightly of the riches of His kindness and tolerance and patience, not knowing that the kindness of God leads you to repentance?" There is a risk to reward ratio that we need to think about when we consider doing that which we know is unpleasing to God. We are hurtful to ourselves and to our God. What is the reward we are going to get compared to the risks that we are taking? If we look at the reward, it is usually just for a moment; it is a temporal, fading reward. The risk is jeopardizing relationships with others, with those that love us most dearly, and more importantly, with God. Is that risk worth a short, fleeting time of gratification? So many times we don't look at the risk being taken but only at the reward. When there is a violation of God's will, the reward, when measured by the risk, would be infinitesimal.

"But because of your stubbornness and unrepentant heart you are storing up wrath for yourself in the day of wrath and revelation of the righteous judgment of God, who *will render to every man according to his deeds*:' to those who by perseverance in doing good seek for glory and honor and immortality, eternal life; but to those who are selfishly ambitious and do not obey the truth, but obey unrighteousness, wrath and indignation. There will be tribulation and distress for every soul of man who does evil, of the Jew first and also of the Greek…" (Romans 2:5–9). In verse 9, Paul goes back to the theme of the book, and we can begin to realize how great the power of the Gospel is to overcome the resistance of wickedness. The glory and the power of the Gospel also reward good that is done by bringing honor and peace to everyone who lives by the directives of the Gospel. This is noted in the following verses.

Let's look at Romans 2:10–16, "…but glory and honor and peace to every man who does good, to the Jew first and also to the Greek. For there is no partiality with God. For all who have sinned without the Law will also perish without the Law…" (referring to the Greek) "…and all who have sinned under the Law will be judged by the Law…" (referring to the Jews) "…for it is not the hearers of the Law who are just before God, but the doers of the Law will be justified. For when Gentiles who do not have the Law do instinctively…" (Now, remember that we already talked about how people have this deep, intuitive desire to worship.) "…the things of the Law, these, not having the Law, are a law to themselves, in that they show the work of the Law written in their hearts, their conscience bearing witness and their thoughts alternately accusing or else defending themselves, on the day when, according to my gospel, God will judge the secrets of men through Christ Jesus."

If a person never violated his own conscience, it would be possible for a person outside of the Law and outside of grace to reach heaven. The only person in the flesh that ever did that was conceived by the Holy Spirit and crucified by the very people who could not handle that type of righteousness, so while the possibility may be there, the probability is not.

Although this next section addresses the Jew, pay close attention because it also applies to the Christian. Romans 2:17–23, "But if you bear the name 'Jew…'" (This refers to those who were under a covenant relationship with God. In principle, we can put in the word "churchianity" as it applies to the church today.) "…and rely upon the Law and boast in God…" (We rely upon grace and boast in God.) "…and know His will and approve the things that are essential, being instructed out of the Law…" (We would insert "Gospel" for "Law.") "…and are confident that you yourself are a guide to the blind, a light to those who are in darkness…" (Don't we feel confident in that area as Christians? So did the Jews.) "…a corrector of the foolish, a teacher of the immature, having in the Law…" (or Gospel—if you want to bring it up to date into this covenant) "…the embodiment of knowledge and of the truth…" (Don't we as a congregation and as individuals strive for knowledge and truth? Absolutely!) "…you, therefore, who teach another, do you not teach yourself? You who preach that one should not steal, do you steal? You who say that one should not commit adultery, do you commit adultery? You who abhor idols, do you rob temples? You who boast in the Law…" (or in the Gospel) "…through your breaking the Law, do you dishonor God?" (Of course, we do!)

One of the elders of the home church where I was baptized, married, and ordained, was the depot master at the local railroad station back during WWII. My dad drove a truck back and forth to the railroad station, where he would unload the truck from North American and Douglas Aviation Company about four or five miles away. When I started going to the church, my dad wasn't too happy about it. When I approached him about his relationship with God, he said, "Ted, I think I have a better relationship with God then one of your elders."

I said, "Oops, what do you mean?"

He said, "Well, your elder who is the railroad master tweaks the manifests from the railcars that the government sent and manipulates those so that at the end of the year his bonus was absolutely fantastic." Now, before the Depression my dad was an accountant, a bookkeeper, and so he was aware of these things. He continued, "Why should I belong to a church that has a leadership like that?"

Powerful question, isn't it? It would behoove each one of us to conduct our lives and our affairs in the light of God's will, for others who are not in Christ are watching us. We must behave in such a way that first we are working for God and second we are working for an employer or supervising employees. Dad and I got around that difficulty, and in time, one of the greatest thrills of my life was when, with my own two hands, I baptized my dad into Christ. Bless the Lord, oh my soul.

As we move on, Romans 2:24 says, "For '*the name of god is blasphemed among the gentiles because of you,*' just as it is written." Duane Hess, a member of one of my classes, made this comment, "The Jews took liberties because they felt they were chosen. They were not chosen because they were better than anyone else but because God wanted to use them to bring His Son into the world through their bloodline. This is what made them head and shoulders above their contemporaries. Most of their problems were of arrogance, not giving the glory to God but assuming it for themselves." There are certain Christian groups and certain people who act in the same fashion. I was at a dinner with very, very dear friends of mine. They thought that I was spiritually weak because I did not receive the same spiritual experience they received. This is the same attitude the Jews had. We can have this same attitude as the Jews did toward others, if we are not careful. Suppose people come into our place of worship, our fellowship, and they are not dressed very well, don't smell very good, don't have social graces, or don't raise their hands when they sing or even say an "amen." Our tendency might be to pull back instead of reaching out. This is what Paul is referring to here. Exercising our spiritual gifts does not give us the authority to occupy a position of spiritual superiority. May we all rise to the level of a bond-servant and not fall into the depth of judgmental hypocrisy. There are too many empty pews in too many congregations because we feel too good to reach out to those who we feel are beneath us.

Paul goes on to discuss both the Jews and Gentiles in Romans 2:25–26: "For indeed circumcision is of value if you practice the Law; but if you are a transgressor of the Law, your circumcision has become uncircumcision. If therefore the uncircumcised man keeps the requirements of the Law, will not his uncircumcision be regarded as circumcision?" The answer is "yes." Colossians 2:11–19 says, "and in Him you were also circumcised with a circumcision made without hands, in the removal of the body of the flesh by the circumcision of Christ; having been buried with Him in baptism, in which you were also raised up with Him through faith in the working of God, who raised Him from the dead. When you were dead in your transgressions and the uncircumcision of your flesh, He made you alive together with Him, having forgiven us all our transgressions, having canceled out the certificate of debt consisting of decrees against us, which was hostile to us; and He has taken it out of the way, having nailed it to the cross. When He had disarmed the rulers and authorities, He made a public display of them, having triumphed over them through Him. Therefore let no one act as your judge in regard to food or drink or in respect to a festival or a new moon or a Sabbath day—things which are a mere shadow of what is to come; but the substance belongs to Christ. Let no one keep defrauding you of your prize by delighting in self-abasement and the worship of the angels, taking his stand on visions he has seen, inflated without cause by his fleshly mind, and not holding fast to the head, from whom the entire body, being supplied and held together by the joints and ligaments, grow with a growth which is from God."

The concept of a birth right into God's family is brought out again in Galatians 3:26–29, which says, "For you are all sons of God through faith in Christ Jesus. For all of you who were baptized into Christ have clothed yourselves with Christ. There is neither Jew nor Greek, there is neither slave nor free man, there is neither male nor female; for you are all one in Christ Jesus. And if you belong to Christ, then you are Abraham's offspring, heirs according to promise." We

ROMANCE WITH ROMANS

are clothed with Christ, for as many of us as have been baptized into Christ Jesus did put Him on. And just as verse 28 says, there is no distinction—all who are in Christ belong to Christ.

Boy, you can see that we are the circumcised children of God—not of the flesh but of the heart. That encompasses the whole transition of Old to New Testament, the taking of the physical application of the Old Testament and converting it to the spiritual application of the New Testament. Romans 2:27–29 says, "And he who is physically uncircumcised, if he keeps the Law, will he not judge you who though having the letter of the Law and circumcision are a transgressor of the Law? For he is not a Jew who is one outwardly, nor is circumcision that which is outward in the flesh; but he is a Jew who is one inwardly; and circumcision is that which is of the heart, by the Spirit, not by the letter; and his praise is not from men, but from God."

QUESTIONS AND DISCUSSION FOR POWER TO OVERCOME THE SINS OF THE JEWS

1. Discuss whether God's main issue with the Jews was their theology or their hypocrisy (verse 3).

2. Name the ways the Jews were accused of hypocrisy. (See verses 1–8.)

3. Today, who are the chosen people of God? (Note Galatians 3:27–29.)

4. Can hypocrisy be seen in "churchianity" today? How?

5. Does our being under grace allow us to be excused from hypocrisy? (See verses 11–12.)

6. Are there ways in which your congregation practices hypocrisy? And you?

7. What circumcision does God recognize as valid? (See verses 28–29.)

8. How are we circumcised spiritually? (See Colossians 2:9–12.)

Addressing Objections

Romans 3:1–20

Hey, wait a minute! The Jews of Jesus' day thought and the Christians of today think that being a child of God brings all kinds of advantages, but we sure don't see them coming to the surface in chapter two. What's going on?

26

Let's look at chapter 3. Romans 3:1(parenthetical statements mine): "Then what advantage has the Jew (or Christian)? Or what is the benefit of circumcision (or Baptism)?" Good questions, don't you think? If it doesn't make any difference in the end, then what is the advantage? Did a Jew have an advantage? Paul responds, "Great in every respect." Notice how Paul develops this. "First of all, that they were entrusted with the oracles of God. What then? If some did not believe, their unbelief will not nullify the faithfulness of God, will it? May it never be! Rather, let God be found true, though every man be found a liar, as it is written, '*that you may be justified in your words, and prevail when you are judged*'" (Romans 3:2–4).

Romans 3:5 continues, "But if our unrighteousness demonstrates the righteousness of God, what shall we say? The God who inflicts wrath is not unrighteous, is He? (I am speaking in human terms.)" Should God pour out His wrath? Some may call that an unjust thing; however, we cannot come to that conclusion. Verses 6–9 say, "May it never be! For otherwise, how will God judge the world? But if through my lie the truth of God abounded to His glory, why am I also still being judged as a sinner? And why not say (as we are slanderously reported and as some affirm that we say), 'Let us do evil that good may come'? Their condemnation is just. What then? Are we better than they? Not at all; for we have already charged that both Jews and Greeks are all under sin…"

Paul goes on to quote extensively from the Old Testament in verses 10–18, (see Romans 3:10–18) since he is directing these comments to the Jews to validate the soundness of his logic. Then he continues (Romans 3:19–20), "Now we know that whatever the Law says, it speaks to those who are under the Law, that every mouth may be closed, and all the world may become accountable to God; because by the works of the Law no flesh will be justified in His sight; for through the Law comes the knowledge of sin." One of the purposes of the Law was to be an escort to Christ. That's the bottom line for God giving the Law. The Jewish nation was the vehicle used by God to perform this act. And in spite of their behavior, God was faithful to His promise!

Let's take a look at where we have been. Apart from the Law, we go forward to the Gospel. "I am not ashamed of the Gospel, for it is the power of God unto salvation…" How great is that power? It is greater than the greatness of sin. How great, how divisive, how demeaning, how universal is sin? We saw it spelled out in the latter part of the first chapter and in the entire second chapter. Provocative questions are asked in the third chapter, which deals with sin. In light of all of this sin, whether it was committed by those living in the 1st century or in the 21st century, the power of the righteousness of God is being revealed. We are going to see the other side of the coin in the following lessons.

For us to appreciate the real power of the Gospel, we need to realize the terrible power of sin. Sin is universal, to the non-religious as well as the religious. It casts mankind into acts worse than animals perform. It demonstrates to the religious that when they depart from their purpose and become legalistic to others while involved in the same sins, they stand condemned. Jesus took note of this during His ministry (see Matthew 23).

Where shall we go but to the Lord? Lost are we all! Now we are ready for the thrill of grace and the power of the Gospel, to which we fix our hope. What a blessing is placed before us as we continue in our love affair with the book of Romans.

QUESTIONS AND DISCUSSION FOR ADDRESSING OBJECTIONS

1. What advantages did the Jews have that Christians have today? (See verses 1–4.)

2. How is "speaking in human terms" applicable to Christians today? (See verse 5.)

3. Is the judgment of God based upon what the majority feel is righteousness? Defend your answer. (See verses 6–7.)

4. Have both the Jews and Gentiles been charged with sin? (See verse 9.)

5. What is one of the consequences of the Law upon the world? (See verse 19.)

6. Where do we obtain our knowledge of what sin is? (See verse 20.)

7. Why is it that there is no justification through the Law? (See verse 20.)

8. Would it be fair to apply the principle of the inconsistency of the Jews to "churchianity" today? (See Revelation 2 and 3.)

Chapter 3

CHRIST'S RIGHTEOUSNESS PLUS MAN'S FAITH GAINS SALVATION
ROMANS 3:21–31

Introduction

ROMANS BEGAN WITH Paul introducing himself as a bond-servant and as one called, sent, and commissioned, and hence, an apostle. Paul discussed the fact that Christ was born of the seed of David, the reason why this visit to earth by God was made, and the reason for His death, burial, and resurrection. Paul concludes this glowing introduction by expressing his longing to come to Rome and share the Gospel together with them, so that both he and those at Rome might benefit.

Paul then sets the theme of the book as: the power of the Gospel unto salvation. The righteousness of God is revealed from faith unto faith. Paul illustrates how powerful the Gospel is by showing what the Gospel is going to overcome through the righteousness of Christ.

He addresses the Gentiles first. A Gentile, at the time of Jesus, was anyone who was not a Jew. To the Jews, all Gentiles were considered barbarians, because they were not true believers in God. The Jews viewed all barbarians as dogs. Not the "man's best friend" kind, not the "you can take my wife, you can take my kids, but don't mess with my dog" kind, but the "coyote, varmint, nuisance, get off my property" kind. If Jews really wanted to get mean and nasty, they referred to Gentiles as "swine," which was about as low as you could get in the esteem of the Jewish people in Jesus' day. Remember the parable of the prodigal son in Luke 15:11–32? Remember the son who left home with his inheritance? Where did he wind up? He wound up feeding the hogs and eating the residue that was fit only for swine. That is as low as a Jew can get in his social status. He was so low he could have walked under a snake's belly, in a rut, with a top hat on.

After Paul discussed the plight of the Gentiles and their universal need to come to the righteousness of God, he pointed out that they were without excuse because God had given them a conscience. Had they obeyed that conscience, they would have been all right; but they didn't.

The Jew reading what Paul wrote regarding the Gentiles, might start to become more pietistic in his thinking. So, in response to this notion, Paul really lays it on the Jews in the second chapter and continues on through to the middle of the third, as we have noted. He says that just having the Law does not justify you. It is not the hearers but the doers of the Law who are justified, and since no one could perfectly do the Law, no one was justified by the Law. He pours it on so much that they ask this question: What advantage is there then to being a Jew?

Let's draw a parallel with that. What if God said, "Alright, you Christians, I am going to invite other people who aren't Christians into heaven, and you are just going to have to learn to live with that?" Would we say, "What advantage is there to being a Christian?" The Jews, with the providential watch care of God, had the will of God written out for them, and they had a standard of living that was far above their contemporaries. It was of great advantage to be a Jew, and it is now a greater advantage to be a Christian, even if at the last moment God does rake in everybody else. I would be happy to be a Christian just for the benefits that are here in this life. And remember, heaven is thrown in. But it still comes down to the bottom line—we are not justified by the Law. Jews, you can't get to heaven from your relationship with the Law. Well, then, from where is justification going to come? Where and how? That is the power of the Gospel, for it declares the where and how of our obtaining salvation.

From Romans 3:21 to the conclusion of the eleventh chapter of Romans, we are going to be dealing with this matter of righteousness and justification as seen in the proclamation and in the living Gospel—that which Jesus accomplished and in our proclamation of it. We have seen the tremendous stranglehold that Satan and sin have on all facets of society. Now we are going to understand how the Gospel's power can overcome the plight of the Gentiles and the plight of the Jews. We are ready to embark upon a fantastic adventure!

Righteousness and Faith

Romans 3:21–22

We begin with Romans 3:21: "But now apart from the Law the righteousness of God has been manifested, being witnessed by the Law and the Prophets..." This is important! Christianity is not a stepchild of Judaism. It is a new covenant. The old covenant is finished. I am very comfortable with and appreciate the words of Jesus on the cross when he said, "It is finished" (John 19:30). He was referring to the old contract being fulfilled and complete, not to his life, for that certainly was not finished—not to his influences, not to his ministry, for those things were not finished. They are still with us today; bless the Lord, O my soul! But that which was finished was the old covenant—not destroyed, not abandoned, but completed. It is like making a final payment on the mortgage of your house. Now you are ready to sell that old thing and go back into hock for a new and better house. It's the same with a car. If you have had it for five years, it probably has 250,000 miles on it. It is not worth a plug nickel, but it is finally paid for, and what do you do? You get rid of the old shebang for safety's sake and go back into a new covenant or a new contract. That is exactly what is happening here. We are in a new contract; the old one has been completed. Paul is able to say "apart from the Law" you don't hang on to the old contract once the last payment has been made. The last payment of the Law was paid at the cross.

There are eternal principles that are given in the Law and are incorporated, and even embellished upon, in the New Covenant. An illustration of this is given in five distinct ways in Jesus' Sermon on the Mount. Here Jesus upgrades the behavioral requirements of the Law with requirements of grace and love:

- The first upgrade begins in Matthew 5:21–24, which says, "…You shall not commit murder… But I say to you that everyone who is angry with his brother shall be guilty… Therefore if you are presenting your offering at the alter, and there remember that your brother has something against you…first be reconciled to your brother, and then come and present your offering."
- The second upgrade begins in Matthew 5:27–30: "…You shall not commit adultery… everyone who looks on a woman to lust for her has committed adultery with her already in his heart…for it is better for you that one of the parts of your body perish, than for your whole body to go into hell."
- The third upgrade begins in Matthew 5:33–34. Jesus continues, "…You shall not make false vows, but shall fulfill your vows to the Lord! But I say to you, make no oath at all…"
- The fourth upgrade begins in Matthew 5:38–41, which says, "You have heard it said, 'An eye for an eye, and a tooth for a tooth.'…whosoever slaps you on your right cheek, turn to him the other also…And whoever shall force you to go one mile, go with him two."
- The fifth upgrade begins in Matthew 5:43–44: "'…You shall love your neighbor and hate your enemy.' But I say to you, love your enemies and pray for those who persecute you."

In addition to these upgrades in Matthew, you can look at the whole book of Hebrews. It takes the physical events of the Old Testament and upgrades them to the spiritual dynamics of the New Testament.

Let's look at Romans 3:21 again: "But now apart from the Law, the righteousness of God has been manifested, being witnessed by the Law and the Prophets…" It has been made known, declared—there is nothing secret to anybody, any nation, any class of people, any society, or any ethnic background. Others are no longer considered dogs; if they have been kissed by God's grace and brought to Christ, they are justified through Him. It is no longer a national situation but a situation of the heart.

"...the righteousness of God has been manifested, being witnessed by the Law and the Prophets," In Romans 3:21, Galatians 3:24 it tells us that the Law was an escort, a tutor, a chaperone to guide us to Christ. That was the purpose of the Law. It is now a time when the people of God can have this love affair with Him through Jesus Christ. The principles of the Law are carried over in total to the New Covenant. It is just the manner or the procedure of execution of the covenants that have changed. Animal sacrifice changed to God being the sacrifice, a Sabbath day's rest changed to a whole life of rest in Christ. When we become Christians, we are on our Sabbath. For further study on this, the forth chapter of Hebrews contains a great parallel between the Sabbath day and what Jesus said in Matthew. Matthew 11:28 says, "Come to me all who are weary and heavy laden, and I will give you rest." The Sabbath was for rest, and when we come to Jesus, we enter into that spiritual Sabbath.

Romans 3:22 says, "...even the righteousness of God through faith in Jesus Christ for all those who believe; for there is no distinction." Righteousness is obtained through faith. There is a theological debate as to whether Jesus is the subject or object of our faith. If it is our faith in Christ that brings righteousness, then He is the object of our faith. If faith is subjective, then it is the faith of Christ that what He was doing would bring about righteousness, that we would accept. In other words, that He would have faith in mankind to accept His righteousness. But you know what? At the end of the day, it is all the same. There is righteousness in Christ, whether it is His faith that induced it for us or our faith because of our response to what He did that induces righteousness to us. The bottom line is that we shall be justified by His righteousness through faith—"...for there is no distinction..." This last phrase leads me to lean towards it being objective and thinking that it is our faith in Christ that brings righteousness; and I feel comfortable with that.

QUESTIONS AND DISCUSSION FOR RIGHTEOUSNESS AND FAITH

1. How can the righteousness of God come apart from the Law? (See verse 22.)

2. How is God's righteousness obtained? (See verse 22.)

3. Give the reason for the righteousness of God.

4. How is the righteousness of God obtained and maintained?

The Need, the Remedy

Romans 3:23–31

Romans 3:23–24: "…for all have sinned and fall short of the glory of God, being justified as a gift by His grace through the redemption which is in Christ Jesus…" This has to be one of the most powerful verses in the New Testament; it is certainly one of the most powerful verses in the book of Romans. Let me bring to your attention the beauty and the depth of this verse. To be justified means, as David of old said, "that our transgressions will be removed as far as the east is from the west" (Psalm 103:12). In Christ, this prophecy was completed, and our sins have been removed to where they shall never be recorded. In legal terms, the record of our sins has been expunged, wiped clean. No one will ever be able to go back and find a record of our past misdeeds. Think of that—justification is an expunging of the record. The blood of Christ not only cleansed us from our sins but also erased them. So God sees in us Christ. Paul was able to say in Colossians 1:27, "…Christ in you the hope of Glory."

This justification is a gift. We couldn't earn it by keeping the Law; we couldn't earn it by keeping our conscience. If justification is going to come, it is going to come as a gift—a free gift. But I want to make definite delineation between the subjective and objective case. It is a free gift and is in the subjective and not the objective case. God (the subject) was not indebted; He was not bound; He was not obligated. He was not required to do anything for man but to pour out his wrath upon man, whether Jew or Gentile, for the violation of conscience or the violation of His Law. So God, without any obligation, moved without any motive other than His love. God so loved the world that He gave the gift. The free gift of grace is subjective. It is that which God gave willingly, desirously, and passionately because of the great love He has for us. That grace is demonstrated through redemption, which is in Christ Jesus. Romans 3:24: "being justified as a gift by His grace through the redemption which is in Christ Jesus." We sing that great old song, "Redeemed! How I love to proclaim it. Redeemed by the blood of the Lamb." Now, if you are going to redeem something, you are going to have to pay something of greater value for that object you are going to redeem.

My dad lived with us for about 15 years. What a blessed experience that was. He was great at woodworking, and he would make little things. He made a toy box for one of my daughters. Though my father was not an offspring of Abraham, he still had many of the traits of the ancient Jews, and he believed in applying paint that was a coat of many colors. There was one strip of blue, one of yellow, one of red, and one of green. It was really bright and unique. He gave the box to my elder daughter. Dawna loved that thing. When she got older and was in high school, the box was finally relegated out to the garage. Leanna, our youngest, needed to raise money to go to Hawaii with her high school choir group. The group planned a huge yard sale. Leanna gathered up all the discarded stuff in the house, and one of the things that she gathered was the box. Now it wasn't hers, but it wasn't in use, so she took it down thinking somebody would want it.

Well, Dawna came home, and she was really distressed. Dawna is the achiever, and my other two kids are a bit blasé. They don't care what is going on as long as it is going. Dawna was more than a little upset and said, "Dad what are we going to do?"

I replied, "OK, let's go down to where they are having this rummage sale, and let's see if it is still there." So, down we go. And sure enough, the box was there. I explained to the lady that the box was brought by mistake, it wasn't Leanna's to give, and it belonged to my other daughter.

Dawna added, "Yeah, that's my box. May we please take it home?"

They said, "No, no. It is a part of the rummage sale. You can redeem it for $9.00."

Anyway, I had to redeem that box. The point is that I had to pay for something that already once was mine, and it had to be of a greater value than what it was worth, for nobody else would pay $9.00 for it. That is exactly what redemption is. God redeemed, at an immense price, that which already belonged to Him. It was taken by Satan, who was not the author of it or creator of it, and thankfully, God chose to buy it back. That's redemption!

Now remember how I said that in order to redeem something a price greater than that which the object is worth must be paid? What is of greater value than man? Mankind is the last of God's creation. There has been nothing physically created since mankind. The only new creation is a spiritual creation that comes along through the New Covenant. We become a new creature in Christ, but it is an internal thing. What is of greater value than man? Only God; so to redeem us, God paid the price. When you come to this word "ransom" or "redemption," think of that. We are redeemed by the only entity that is of greater value than man, and that is God himself (1 Peter 1:18–19).

Being justified by our redemption causes the record of our sin to be expunged as a gift, not given out of obligation, but freely given through Jesus Christ, for He is our redemption. Boy! What a powerful verse!

Romans 3: 25 says, "…whom God displayed publicly…" Jesus didn't go to some monastery or down with the Essenes to Qumran to hibernate there at the top of the Dead Sea. His whole life and ministry was public. The people came and followed Him by the hundreds and by the thousands, not because of his earthly nobility or His reign of power, but because they saw in Him all that they wanted to be. They saw in Him that which was truly exceptional. They saw in Him the very presence of God. In Matthew 16:13, Jesus asked His disciples this question: "Who do people say that the Son of Man is?" They replied in verse 14: "And they said, 'Some say John the Baptist; some, Elijah; and others Jeremiah, or one of the prophets.'" In verse 15, He asked them, "But who do you say that I am?" Peter answered in verse 16, saying, "…You are the Christ, the Son of the Living God." Upon that truth there is built a means by which we can become a part of His family.

So we have been redeemed in a public display as a propitiation for our sins (some translations use the term "atonement"). The word propitiation has a little bit different meaning than atonement, because it means that there is a covering over, a tenting. Christ is the one who covers over the sin so that God does not see our sin, for that record is expunged by its being covered in the righteous blood of Jesus. Jesus' blood is righteous on two accounts: 1) He was conceived by a seed that did not have sin inherent within it (Luke 1:35). 2) He was tempted in every way, just like we are, yet He was without sin (Hebrews 4:15). There was no inherent death in Christ; the death He died was not just a hastening of the ultimate end of Jesus. Rather, it was the giving of Himself as a gift of grace to redeem us by the covering of precious, holy, unspotted, pure, unsoiled, unmolested blood from its conception to its termination.

Consider this hypothetically—since there was no element of death in Him, Jesus would not have had to die. This perspective adds an extra value, an emphasis to the cross that Christ was hung upon and the death that He died in order that we might be redeemed (see Revelation 5).

Romans 3:25 continues, "…as a propitiation in His blood through faith. This was to demonstrate His righteousness, because in the forbearance of God He passed over the sins previously committed…" Does that mean the sins we previously committed? Absolutely! Hebrews chapter 11 denotes that there are men of faith that are our witnesses. I like to think that the blood of Christ is not bound by a historical event that was just for His day, but that one arm of the cross reaches back to the faithful of the Old Testament as one is coming forward to the faithful of the New. This is exciting. This is really down to the hub, to the real heart and core of our faith; what it means to us; why we believe; why we are willing to give, to sacrifice, and to yield our life to Him because of what He has done. Oh, the marvel of it!

Let's explore the concept of sins committed beforehand going unpunished. Consider John 14:6: "…no one comes to the Father, but through Me," says Jesus. So does that mean no man from that time on, or does that mean no man ever? There is nothing in the Scriptures that brings it down to "from that time on" except our tunnel vision of theology. After all, they had sins then, and they needed to be redeemed. The Old Testament crowd certainly couldn't have true redemption by the blood of goats, bullocks, and sheep. The only redemptive quality they had was in an event that had not yet taken place in man's time; but when it did take place, their faith would be rewarded. The reason for our limitation in this is that we want to bring God back into the confines of our concept of time. It is a natural thing to try to shrink Him into that by which we measure things. But God is beyond those confines, and a day is as a thousand years and a thousand years is a day (2 Peter 3:8). The blood of Christ can reach back 4,000 years as easily as it can reach forward 4,000 years.

Romans 3:26–27: "…for the demonstration, I say, of His righteousness at the present time, so that He would be just and the justifier of the one who has faith in Jesus. Where, then, is boasting? It is excluded. By what kind of law? Of works? No, but by a law of faith." From the cross forward to the present time in which righteousness is to be declared, justification had to be through a gift unmerited. It is a gift of God; it is the righteousness of God. It is apart from the Law. It is redemption bought back with a price, by His blood. No person should boast in being a Christian. He or she is a Christian not by that which he or she deserves but by that which God has given. Now, when we speak about the Law not being able to justify, we are speaking about the Law that God gave to Moses. Does that mean that we are void of law? No we are not void of law. The Law burned by the finger of God upon a rock has no redemptive power, not because the law is weak, for it is not, but because of the weakness of man. Now we live by the law of faith which has been burned in our hearts by the finger of God through the message of grace (2 Cor. 3:2–11).

Saving Faith

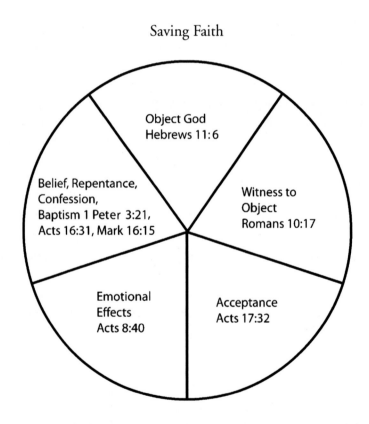

To understand saving faith, we must understand the parameters of faith. They can be represented in a pentagon or circle divided into 5 pieces of pie. The first piece, at the top of the circle, is faith. Faith must have an object. Since we are talking about saving faith, the object would be God (Hebrews 11:6). But to have faith in an object, there must be a witness regarding the object, which is noted in the second piece of the pie (Romans 10:17). The third piece is an acceptance of the witness regarding the object. There are only three things we can do with a witness. We can sneer at it and reject it, need further witnesses before we accept it, or we can accept it. An example of that is seen in Acts 17:32–34. Once a witness is accepted regarding an object, it will have an emotional effect upon us, which is the fourth piece (Acts 8:40). The final piece depicts when that emotion drives us, compels us. It makes us desire to fulfill the dictates of the witness. In the scriptures from 1 Peter 3:21; Acts 16:31; and Mark 16:15, note the word "saved" or "salvation." All of this together leads us back to the first piece of the pie of Saving Faith. None of these are works of the Law given to Moses or the merits of man, but they are our gift by the obedience to faith (Acts 5:32).

Referring to the Law of Moses, Romans 3:28 states, "For we maintain that a man is justified by faith apart from works of the law." There is a need and a place for faith to express itself through obedience to the demands on our faith. Grace is not free in the sense that it doesn't cost us anything. Paul says this in Romans 12:1: "Therefore, I urge you, brethren by the mercies of God, to present your bodies a living and holy sacrifice, acceptable to God, which is your spiritual service of worship."

Romans chapter three concludes with verses 29–31: "Or is God the God of Jews only? Is He not the God of Gentiles also? Yes, of Gentiles also, since indeed God who will justify the circumcised by faith and the uncircumcised through faith is one." It is faith that led them to Christ, the faith that we have in Jesus Christ and through Him. "Do we then nullify the Law through faith? May it never be! On the contrary, we establish the Law." This is how we establish or uphold the law, by embracing Him who completed the Law.

I hope you were blessed by this great passage of Scripture. It is fitting for us to share a brief prayer: *Oh God, may we ever fall more deeply, more earnestly, and more passionately in love with you as we see what you have done for us and recognize the beauty of our redemption in Jesus. For it is in His name we pray. Amen.*

QUESTIONS AND DISCUSSION FOR THE NEED, THE REMEDY

1. What is the meaning of "What is involved in Justification"? (Note the commentary on verse 23.)

2. In what respect is the gift of grace free? (See verse 23.)

3. What is the key principle regarding the word "redeemed"? (See verse 24.)

4. Who or what is of greater value than humans? (See verse 24.)

5. Do we deserve to be Christians? (See verse 27.)

6. Are we under a Law? (Note verse 28.)

7. What are the parameters of the Law of saving faith? (Note Saving Faith diagram.)

Chapter 4

FAITH AS MAN'S REACTION TO GOD'S ACTION OF REDEMPTION
ROMANS 4:1–25

Introduction

THIS FOURTH CHAPTER of the book of Romans is an exciting one. The most beautiful thing we'll see in this chapter is that it folds back to the theme of the book, which we found in Romans 1:16 and 17 (paraphrased): "I am not ashamed of the Gospel, for it is the power of God unto salvation; for there in is revealed the righteousness of God from faith unto faith." The power of the Gospel is going to be centered in the revealing of the righteousness of God. We saw how God revealed His righteousness in the third chapter. We saw a tremendous need, due to the universality of sin, in both Gentiles and Jews. Romans 3:23: "For all have sinned and fall short of the Glory of God," Romans 3:10: " …there is none righteous, not even one." The revealing of righteousness is in Christ Jesus. Remember Romans 3:21 states, "But now apart from the Law the righteousness of God has been manifested, being witnessed by the Law and the prophets."

The question comes: What is the foundational key to the obtaining of righteousness? Paul pretty well negated the fact that it is going to be through the Law. In Romans 3:27 we have this interesting little gem that we were able to pick out, and we found that it is not by the works of the Law of Moses, but by the law of faith. It is so fascinating to think that faith has a law, that faith has parameters. God, the Word, the acceptance, the emotion, and the motivation to obey all apply to a saving faith, but the same principles apply to the maintenance of faith or the growing in faith. See the illustration below, where we compare a saving faith with a growing faith.

Note that the difference is in the fifth sector. Each is driven by the "Emotional Effects." But in the latter figure we see the action of our faith in prayer, faithfulness, and so forth. These are essential to keeping and growing in faith.

Saving Faith   Growing Faith

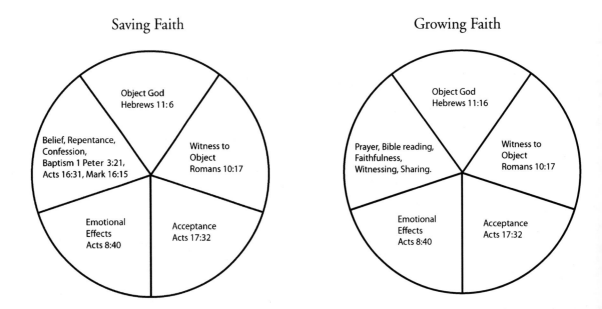

The main difference between the Law of Moses and the law of faith is that the first, the Law of Moses was obeyed out of compulsion, the second, the law of faith is obeyed out of willingness. So this is the law of faith in my meager understanding. I am confident that I haven't as yet even touched the hem of the garment of the meaning and the depth of Romans 3:27, when it says, "…a law of faith." It is a tantalizing, teasing, and fascinating statement.

Justification and Works

Romans 4:1–8

Let's explore how this righteousness that has been revealed in Jesus is acquired.

Paul really is a masterful diplomat. His presentation is appealing and relevant to the Romans and to the Jews. In Romans 4:1 he begins, "What then shall we say that Abraham, our forefather according to the flesh, has found?" The relevance to the Jews is readily seen in this verse. Is Abraham righteous because of his works, or is it because of his faith? Faith, of course, and the appeal to the Jew is this—that Abraham was the forerunner of the Law, the father of the Jewish nation. Many aspects or principles of the Law, one in particular, were mandated of him. It is also relevant to the Romans, who detested the Jewish religion because of its strict moral code and exclusiveness to the keeping of the Law. In the Jews' eyes, their living outside the Law made the Romans nothing more than dogs. So Paul presents the one who preceded the Law, Abraham, who could not have been bound by that future Law, which was not as yet given as the instrument of righteousness. Through Abraham, Paul is providing the instrument for righteousness and elevates the Jewish people beyond the Law and strips away the animosity that the Roman Christians would have because of the Law.

Paul continues (Romans 4:2), "For if Abraham was justified by works, he has something to boast about…" As would we all, but that last phrase really sends it home. He'd have "something to boast about" all right. However, as the rest of the verse says, "…but not before God." We boast in ourselves and in our works, by which people usually judge us. And, fortunately, at our memorial services they only remember the good things, or at least that is the polite thing to do. It is usually because of the works of a person that he or she is elevated. So this philosophy is ingrained within our psyche: work hard and good things will happen. So in reference to the works of the Law, they can boast, but not before God.

We find this in Genesis 15:1–6: "After these things the word of the LORD came to Abram in a vision saying, 'Do not fear, Abram. I am a shield to you; your reward shall be very great.' And Abram said, 'O Lord God, what will You give me, since I am childless and the heir of my house is Eliezer of Damascus?'" (verses 1 and 2). Interpretation: I don't have any children to leave my inheritance to. It is going to some guy over in Damascus. "And Abram said, 'Since You have given no offspring to me, one born in my house is my heir" (verse 3). Interpretation: God, it is all your fault. "Then behold, the word of the LORD came to him, saying, 'This man will not be your heir…'" (verse 4). Interpretation: Eliezer of Damascus is not going to get one single blooming dime out of you. The Lord continues in verses 4 and 5, "'…but one who shall come forth from your own body, he shall be your heir.' And He took him outside and said, 'Now, look toward the heavens, and count the stars, if you are able to count them.' And He said to him, 'So shall your descendants be.'" Here is where Abraham became a righteous man. In the face of all these obstacles, and knowing his own physical limitations, he became a righteous man—because he believed in the Lord. "Then he believed in the Lord; and He reckoned it to him as righteousness" (verse 6).

Like Abraham, when you don't think you have the ability or believe you have the talent, remember that God is not there because of your talent or your ability. It is because of your availability and your believing in the promises that He has made. When a congregation thinks that they are childless or they don't have enough people or they can't do it or they don't have enough money or it can't be done, but God still says to do it and they go ahead and do it, then it will be reckoned unto them for righteousness. The principle is not unique to Abraham. It's as applicable to a corporate group as it is to the individuals who make up that corporate group. Faith, trusting in the relevance of God's Word to the particulars at hand, is that which causes an individual to be counted as righteous.

Let's get back to Romans 4:3–6. Verses 3 and 4 say, "For what does the Scripture say? '*Abraham believed god, and it was credited to him as righteousness.*' Now to the one who works, his wages are not reckoned as a favor but as what his due." A workingman's wage is not reckoned as a favor, but it is reckoned as his due. It is not the wages of grace that brings salvation. It is the wages of sin that brings death, but grace, the free gift of God brings salvation (Romans 6:23). In other words, by our faith in Jesus we can get into heaven, but we have to work like the devil to miss heaven. It is for our works that a wage is due. But righteousness is not a product of works; it is a product of faith. There are works of growing in faith, and these works are not to gain salvation, but they are the fruit of salvation. "But to the one who does not work, but believes in Him who justifies the ungodly, his faith is reckoned as righteousness, just as David also speaks of the blessings upon the man to whom God reckons righteousness apart from works" (Romans 5–6). We will explore this principle that it is faith that is credited unto us as righteousness in depth in the fifth and sixth chapters.

Psalm 32:1–2 is quoted in the next two verses of Romans. Romans 4:7–8: "'*Blessed are those whose lawless deeds have been forgiven, and whose sins have been covered. Blessed is the man whose sin the lord will not take into account.*'" Oh my. How blessed are we that our lawless deeds have been forgiven and God reckons righteousness to us because of our faith! You and I, by God's grace, and by our faith in that grace, have an account, a balance sheet that is in the black—all the red ink has been expunged.

QUESTIONS AND DISCUSSION FOR JUSTIFICATION AND WORKS

1. If Abraham was justified by works, where could he boast?
   Where could he not boast? (See verse 4.)

2. How was Abraham deemed righteous? (See verse 3.)

3. How do we obtain God's blessings? (See verse 5.)

4. What is the "blessing" that David talks about? (See verses 6–8.)

Justification and Faith

Romans 4:9–12

Romans 4:9 begins with a weighty, weighty question: "Is this blessing then upon the circumcised or upon the uncircumcised also?" Verses 9–11 continue, "…For we say, '*faith was reckoned to abraham as righteousness.*' How then was it credited? While he was circumcised, or uncircumcised? Not while circumcised, but while uncircumcised; and he received the sign of circumcision, a seal of the righteousness of the faith which he had while uncircumcised…" You see circumcision was the seal of the righteousness of faith to the Jewish people. It was a seal that they belonged to the family of God, physically. Circumcision for male children today is done basically for hygienic purposes, unless you are of the Jewish faith. God initially gave it as a seal or a sign that a young boy was a member of the Jewish nation. Unlike standard practice today, circumcision did not take place at a boy's birth, but eight days later. Then he was counted as one of the Jewish members or as part of the Jewish family, and his heritage became invoked. This was the seal God put upon His nation, indicating the boy was a part of the family of God. So the Jews had to realize that Paul basically was speaking to them in verse 10, but he also included the uncircumcised, which obviously incorporated the Romans.

Again, circumcision was a seal to the Jewish people that they belonged to the family of God, physically. Now, the correlation to this is seen in Colossians 2:9–12: "For in Him all the fullness of Deity dwells in bodily form, and in Him you have been made complete, and He is the head over all rule and authority; and in him you were also circumcised with a circumcision made without hands, in the removal of the body of the flesh, by the circumcision of Christ; having been buried with Him in baptism, in which you were also raised up with Him through faith in the working of God, who raised Him from the dead." So circumcision is transformed to baptism as a sign, or a seal, that we are now spiritually born children of God.

Romans 4:11–12: "…so that he might be the father of all who believe without being circumcised, that righteousness might be credited to them, and the father of circumcision to those who not only are of the circumcision, but who also follow in the steps of the faith of our father Abraham which he had while uncircumcised." Paul has taken this same principle and brought the Romans into the family of God. It isn't the dictates or mandates or constant obedience to the Law that will justify us, for this justification came prior to one of the great statements of the Law regarding the identity of God's children through circumcision. Circumcision was performed throughout history, indicating belonging. Circumcision was given by God to Abraham, and it was included by God in the Mosaic Law. Here, in this fourth chapter, we find that the righteousness of faith is His promise to Abraham and his descendants. He was the heir to the world; not through the Law, but through the righteousness of faith obtained prior to any statute of the Law, even the one that identified the Israelites as children of God.

There are those who say, "Ha, ha! Abraham was justified before that seal was given, hence our justification or our righteousness is before our baptism." This is one theological issue that separates a great body of believers. The issue is whether we are saved prior to our baptism and hence baptized because we are saved or whether we are saved as we are involved in baptism. That issue represents two trains of thought in the Christian community, and there are other ramifications within it. I would like to suggest that both are right. How can that be? Our mistake is in the fact that we equate human time with the process of redemption. I don't think it is valid to do that. In our spiritual regeneration, God is not working in accordance with the physical calendar of hours, minutes, and time as we do. God deals with the person's heart, and as that heart has faith in God, that faith becomes the fruition of our salvation. Let us explore a couple scenarios:

1. A man is converted. Is conversion synonymous with salvation? Some say, "No, it is after a person is immersed that he is saved." How do we know the condition of an immersed person's heart any more then we knew the condition of the person's heart that appears to be converted? If God waits until a man dies to judge him, why should we judge him before he dies?
2. Would Abraham still be counted as righteous if he had not done what God had told him to do? His righteousness was acknowledged because faith drove him and motivated him to comply. He gained the righteousness of God, by faith and obedience. The two are inseparable.
3. This is so powerfully stated in Hebrews 11. We have often led people to a false conclusion by assuring them that once they have been dipped, they have been saved. Then we've watched them revert back into the old ways of life, rather than providing the discipleship, compassion, and understanding that would allow them to grow in this faith. This is failing on our part. Instead of really ministering and tending to the lambs that God allows to come into the flock, we do little. Often we do not follow through.

There are particular and unique promises that are associated with baptism that are not found in any other action, just as there were certain promises associated with circumcision that are unique. Some of the promises of baptism are: the forgiveness of our sin and the gift of the Holy Spirit (Acts 2:38). We are sharing with Jesus in his death, burial, and resurrection, and involving ourselves within the blood of Christ (Romans 6:3–7). We are clothed in Jesus, (Galatians 2:27) no longer to be found naked in our sins but to be garbed in His righteousness. Bless the Lord, oh my soul!

God is going to look at the big picture. I wish that all of us could look at salvation in a big picture. This is how God was looking at Abraham when he said, "I reckoned this for righteousness," simply because Abraham believed that he would have an heir. When we believe, there comes a magnificent and growing gestation period in accordance with a person's own heart and in a person's own ability to learn prior to the time of rebirth. As we correlate all of this together, we can have a great deal of unanimity and understanding. If we could have friendly debates, we could embrace one another as being one in Christ, which, after all, is the church, not the building, not the institution. It was to this end that the restoration fathers strove; this unity was what they really had in mind. I dare say that they crossed denominational lines so much that today many of our fellowships would probably disfellowship them for being too inclusive.

One final comment on the issue: Consider God saying in Romans 9:15, "…I will have mercy on whom I have mercy…" With that verse in mind, everything else is pretty much academic. He has given us guidelines, but the bottom line is, it's all in His hands. Whether or not someone has been circumcised or immersed, it's still in God's hands, for He sees the heart of the individual. For us to bicker and quarrel and fight over such things is pretty much foolishness in the light that God is in control of everything anyway. Worse than that, the greatest hope and the greatest opportunity that man has upon this earth is being shattered because of the divisions existing within "churchianity." As a result, people are shying away, because we sit in the seat of judgment rather than in the seat of a proclaimer of mercy and forgiveness.

But consider this question: Is God the author of the Bible or is the Bible the author of God? Is the author confined only to the Bible or is the Bible confined only to God? The answer is obvious: the Bible is confined only to God. If God is confined to the Bible, then he is smaller or at best equal with the Bible, so that which He has created or made has greater power then the Maker. If the Bible is perfect as God has declared it to be—perfect not only in substance but also in the completion of its content—then every promise that God has made in His Word is relative to our relationship with Him; and He is obligated to keep His Word by His holiness. But if God cannot work beyond that, where does the statement "I will have mercy on whom I have mercy" fit? But when working outside of the Bible, God will never work contrary to His inspired Word.

We must appreciate that the assurance of God's promises are in obedience. We have seen incidences in church history that have brought about a change in the mode of baptism. Suppose a guy is seriously ill and can't get immersed. Or suppose he wants to be immersed out somewhere between Cairo and the Gaza strip, and there is no water. He knows this is what God wants him to do and the promises associated with it. Also, he believes in the lordship of Jesus. Before they can get to Gaza, he drops dead from sunstroke. The legalist would say that he would never make it to heaven. I'm not saying that God is going to let him go down the tubes because circumstances kept him from getting to the spiritual circumcision by water. That is a judgment call only God can make. Where there are external circumstances that prevent the convert from completing his obedience, which he dearly desires to do, God will read the heart. This does not excuse those who are not under similar circumstance to forgo their obedience. The exception to the rule never vetoes the rule. But if a person hears the Gospel, is converted, and then just goes along and refuses to finish obedience unto salvation through baptism, then I think, according to the Scriptures (Matthew 28:18–20; Acts 2:38; Acts 8:30–39; Romans 6:3–7; Galatians 3:27–29; 1 Peter 3:21 to name a few) he may be on pretty dangerous ground.

There is no direct promise in the Scriptures that a person has joined Jesus at his death, burial, and resurrection, except through baptism. The righteousness is of faith, and faith is an inward action. Baptism is an outward action. Repentance is an inward action. Confession is an outward action. All outward actions, to have any validity, are dependent upon what inwardly has gone on before. A person won't repent and turn to God unless he or she realizes who God is and his or her great personal need. Faith was reckoned unto Abraham because he believed that he would bear an heir. Even though by having intercourse with Hagar he broke that faith, it did not deter God from keeping His promise. God still maintained His promise. We will see how that faith overrode his disobedience, even following his initial acceptance as being righteous. This gives us hope that when we stumble and fall and flop, God can recover us. Look at Psalm 107, where time after time it shows the depth to which man has fallen, but when he cries out to the Lord, God's grace is greater than man's errors. Bless the Lord, oh my soul!

When fishing, I don't see the fish until after I hook it; but once I hook one, I prefer to eat mine clean, as it makes it a little more palatable. It is faith that has us hooked. We have the cleansing process as the acceptance of the testimony given to us by God, which brings about faith that emotionally charges us to do the works of faith that cleanse us (1 Peter 3:21).

QUESTIONS AND DISCUSSION FOR JUSTIFICATION AND FAITH

1. Was Abraham regarded as righteous before he was circumcised? (See verse 10.)

2. His circumcision was a seal of what? Obtained how? (See verse 11.)

3. What is the importance of Abraham's being declared righteous prior to his circumcision? (See verse 10.)

The Test of Faith

Romans 4:13–25

Now let's look at Romans 4:13–16. Verse 13 says, "For the promise to Abraham or to his descendants that he would be heir of the world was not through the Law, but through the righteousness of faith." The righteousness of faith was going to cause the people to be heirs. Our faith in the revealed righteousness of Jesus and the matter of faith allows us to be heirs of God (Romans 3:21–22). "For if those who are of the Law are heirs, faith is made void and the promise is nullified…" (Verse 14). It is impossible for the Jews, who are under the Law, while under the Law to be heirs. Why? Because they have violated the Law. "…for the Law brings about wrath, but where there is no law, there also is no violation. For this reason it is by faith, in order that it may be in accordance with grace, so that the promise will be guaranteed to all the descendants, not only to those who are of the Law, but also to those who are of the faith of Abraham who is the father of us all…" (verses 15–16). The Law was an escort, a tutor to lead us up to Christ Jesus. This thought is developed in Galatians 3:13–29. Righteousness is brought about by faith. But faith is more than acceptance; it is the applying of that acceptance to the conveyance, Jesus Christ, which leads us to the goal of being a part of God's family. Galatians 3:29 states, "And if you belong to Christ, then you are Abraham's descendents, heirs according to the promise." Pretty nifty!

Romans 4:17: "(as it is written, '*a father of many nations have I made you*') in the presence of Him whom he believed, even God, who gives life to the dead and calls into being that which does not exist." So we were the called into being. We were called by Christ, by that seed which we accept; and by acceptance, we become a part of the family of God in a mature manner relative to those under the Law. Paul continues (verse 18): "In hope against hope he believed, so that he might become a father of many nations according to that which had been spoken, '*so shall your descendants be.*'" Faith is accepting that which is beyond our ability to perform so God's promise might be kept. Let me rephrase that statement. Faith is the accepting of that which we cannot perform but that God has promised to do. If we must rationalize everything in accordance with our ability to perform, then we are back under the old Law, whether Jew or Gentile. We must place our trust and our ability to perform in the promise that God has made us His heirs. It's the only way that promise can be appreciated. Now this same principle will filter down into other areas and attitudes of our Christian life and living. Paul uses a physical illustration of the bringing about of the seed of promise through Isaac as a "type" to the spiritual promise we have with God. We need also to consider the ability of Abraham and Sarah. Romans 4:18–19 says, "In hope against hope he believed, so that he might become father of many nations according to that which had been spoken, '*so shall your descendants be.*' Without becoming weak in faith he contemplated his own body, now as good as dead since he was about a hundred years old, and the deadness of Sarah's womb…" His body was quite old as far as child bearing was concerned; Sarah's womb had never been alive in that regard. There was no possibility for either of them to have a child. There was no possibility for them to fulfill the promise of God by their own endeavors. There is no possibility for us to fulfill the promises of God in our own ability. We must believe on that which God will provide.

Romans 4:20: "…yet, with respect to the promise of God, he did not waver in unbelief…" Abraham tried to change the mechanics of it, but he still believed in the fact that the promise would be fulfilled. Some might construe that as unbelief, but I think it was a strong belief in the promise of God. Abraham just didn't understand how it could be done without his intervening. And boy, if that isn't perfectly human! Imagine saying to God, "You can't keep your promise unless we get involved"; and yet we do that all the time. What we need to appreciate is that a strong, strong faith will induce us to perform God's will in God's way. Even though Abraham and Sarah were both impotent and incompetent, they nonetheless exercised the opportunity to perform so a son could be conceived. It was there that God intervened.

Verses 20–21 continue: "…but grew strong in faith, giving glory to God, and being fully assured that what God had promised, He was able also to perform." There is one of the greatest classical illustrations and applications that we could possibly hope for of our faith in Jesus Christ! "Therefore 'IT WAS ALSO CREDITED (some translations say reckoned) TO HIM AS RIGHTEOUSNESS.' Now not for his sake only was it written that it was credited to him, but for our sake also, to whom it will be credited (reckoned), as those who believe in Him…" (Romans 4:22–24).

Notice what it is that we are to believe:

- Verse 24: "…who raised Jesus our Lord from the dead,"
- Verse 25: "He who was delivered over because of our transgressions,…"
- Verse 25: "…and was raised because of our justification."

Some translations use the word "for"—"for transgressions" and "for justifications"—rather than "because." Let's read it that way: "He who was delivered over for our transgressions, and was raised for our justification." There in that verse is the crux of the faith that leads to justification. For it is in this faith that righteousness is acknowledged. This is the power of the Gospel that leads unto salvation; therein is revealed the righteousness of God from faith unto faith. Remember that is the premise of Romans, as set out in 1:16–17. We saw righteousness was accounted through faith in the promises of God. We saw righteousness being given to us through His promise in the area where we failed ourselves.

QUESTIONS AND DISCUSSION FOR THE TEST OF FAITH

1. How could faith and the promise of righteousness be made void? (See verses 13–14.)

2. What was called into being that did not exist? (See verse 17.)

3. Why was Jesus raised from the dead? (See verses 24–25.)

4. What obstacle did Abraham's faith have to overcome? (See verse 19.)

5. His faith was the pathway to _____.(See verses 20–21.)

6. Jesus was raised from the dead that by _____ we might be _____. (See verse 25.)

Chapter 5

GOD'S RIGHTEOUSNESS IS A GIFT OF GRACE
ROMANS 5:1–21

Introduction

IN CHAPTER FOUR we began to get an appreciation of the depth of grace. Chapter five begins with the word "therefore," which indicates the effects of the thoughts of chapter four are being continued.

Peace with God

Romans 5:1–11

Romans 5:1: "Therefore, having been justified by faith, we have peace with God through our Lord Jesus Christ…" The fact that we are justified by faith, resulting in our finding peace with God, which is accomplished through Jesus Christ, is established in chapter four. The Law brought about warfare internally with the Jews. But now we have peace instead of warfare.

There is often a battle when we lay our head down upon the pillow at night and before we zonk out, recapping the events of the day. We may say, "Gee, did I do more good things than bad?" If so, the scale weighs in our direction, and we can sleep in peace. But if in all honesty we say, "Whoops! I did more bad things than good today," these events keep replaying in our minds. We toss and turn, counting sheep in a vain effort to find sleep. We watch the hours of the night drag by as we anguish over our own sin. That's the difference between Law and grace. With grace there is peace in the heart—peace that passes all comprehension. It is a peace that is brought about by faith regardless of the circumstances surrounding us, whether physical, spiritual, intellectual, or emotional. The Lord Jesus Christ will place a peace in us as we entrust our lives to Him.

Note the adjective "Lord" that describes Jesus Christ. While it is associated with the whole proper name of Jesus, Lord Jesus Christ, "Lord" nonetheless is a descriptive word regarding Jesus. It describes Him as being the owner and controller and master of our lives and our hearts. We have surrendered and submitted ourselves to God even though we don't know how in the world we are ever going to accomplish His will. Then we look to the Lord and Savior Jesus Christ, for in Him is found the redeeming quality of His blood that paid for our sins. The death, burial, and resurrection demonstrate the power with which He raised us up, and because of our faith in His grace, we have our salvation. To my knowledge, whenever the words "Savior" and "Lord" are used together as a description of Jesus, the word "Lord" always precedes the word "Savior." I don't know of a scripture where it says that He is "Savior and Lord." He is "Lord and Savior." This phrase indicates His authority and our yielding of our authority to His lordship. Once we have yielded to that authority, then the saving power of Jesus can find access to our hearts.

Did you know that faith is but an introduction to grace? Romans 5:2 says, "...through whom also we have obtained our introduction by faith into this grace in which we stand; and we exult in hope of the glory of God." Faith is not the acquiring of a total appreciation of the fullness of God's grace. As far as bringing us into a saving relationship with Him, YES! If the fullness and the perfection of His grace would be obtained upon our acceptance of Christ, then how would we find more grace down the line when we need it? And boy, do we ever need it! So saving faith is but an introduction to God's grace, and hence, that introduction brings an appreciation of the righteousness that God poured out Himself, resulting in our justification because of His grace. Do I believe in the second work of grace? I sure do. There is the constant work of grace within our lives as long as the intent of our hearts is to make Jesus the Lord of our lives.

Do we stumble? Do we fall? Yeah, it happens all the time. Are we to be punished to hell because of it? If we are under the Law, yes; but if we are under the law of faith, no. We then have an introduction to grace, and that grace keeps rolling out. If once we have been introduced to grace we take a stand, then that stand brings about in us a great hope. And our hope brings inner peace.

"And not only this, but we also exult in our tribulations, knowing that tribulation brings about perseverance..." (Romans 5:3). This is a little hard to handle unless we stop and think about it. It is in tribulation that the grace of God becomes so very, very apparent. By tribulation we are brought ever closer to God and are more exalted in grace because of it. Though it is arduous at the time, there is great hope. It develops a stick-to-it attitude, and you will be able to say things like: "God, you have brought me through this automobile accident" or "You got me through this death of a loved one" or "You got me through this illness" or "You brought me through this demise of a relationship" or "You brought me through this financial disaster I faced." "You, God, brought me all the way through."

I personally cannot leave a God like this. A God like this I must cling to; a God like this must be mine now and forevermore! I now have a faith that has perseverance, for it has been tried by tribulation. And I do not regret the tribulation; I exalt in it. In and through tribulation I have a preservation of that grace and a stick-to-it attitude that will develope, and the result is a proven character.

Romans 5:4 continues, "…and perseverance, proven character; and proven character, hope…" This is the constant hope, the trust we put in God. He is our provider! He fulfills His promises beyond our capacity—even as He did for Abraham of old physically, so He shall do for us spiritually. This is the foundation of our hope. Sure, there are going to be really, really difficult times ahead for us. But in those difficult times as well as in those bountiful times, there is infused a steadfast hope. This hope is not a pie-in-the-sky kind of hope, but it is predicated upon personal experience, and more importantly, it is a hope that is predicated upon His promises. "…and hope does not disappoint, because the love of God has been poured out within our hearts through the Holy Spirit who was given to us" (Romans 5:5).

Let's look at a scripture that states when the Holy Spirit is given to us. Acts 5:32 says, "And we are witnesses of these things; and so is the Holy Spirit, whom God has given to those who obey Him." When is this gift presented to us? When we obey Him? When we are obedient to the work of faith we saw in Romans chapter 3? Romans 3:27 says, "Where then is boasting? It is excluded, by what kind of law? Of works? No, but by a law of faith." The work of faith is when we willingly yield to the lordship of Jesus and obey those requests that He makes. So, there is an obedience to be performed. Where can we find an obedience with the promise of the gift of the Holy Spirit? Let's look at Acts 2:38–39: "Peter said to them, 'Repent, and let each of you be baptized in the name of Jesus Christ for the forgiveness of your sins; and you shall receive the gift of the Holy Spirit.' For the promise is for you and your children and for all who are far off, as many as the Lord our God shall call to Himself." Now, let's put this in context. Peter had just finished preaching of the death, burial, and resurrection of Christ, which is the whole foundation and hope of justification and faith. His listeners were pricked in their hearts. They believed, they accepted, and they were hooked. They needed to be cleaned. Once clean, they became vessels in which the Holy Spirit could live, dwell, and abide.

In the righteousness of God, grace is delivered. This is not because of what we have earned or merited. It is because of God's great love for us that He gave to us this divine gift; hence, it was freely given. God was in no way obligated to us, except by His great love for us. This is the way in which we should approach "the free gift of grace." I personally am uncomfortable with the idea that grace is free from the standpoint that we don't have to do anything. It seems after this standpoint is taken there is always an "except," and in that "except," there is work. It takes effort to become a Christian, and it takes effort to remain a Christian. The high cost of grace is seen in the yielding of our lives to the lordship of Jesus, a surrendering without conditions. This takes effort, a crucifying of ourselves, as so beautifully stated by the apostle Paul in Galatians 2:20: "I have been crucified with Christ; and it is no longer I who live, but Christ lives in me, and the life which I now live in the flesh I live by faith in the Son of God, who loved me, and gave Himself up for me."

I was recently introduced to the concept that Jesus was given the Holy Spirit without measure, and consequently, we are given the Holy Spirit with measure. I really feel uncomfortable with this line of reasoning. I feel confident that we are given the Holy Spirit without any reservations. If there is any measure of the working of the Holy Spirit in our lives, it is not due to an inadequacy or apportionment of the Holy Spirit, it is due to an inadequacy of our yielding. Let's put the ball in the right court. So why don't we have the same manifestations that they had on the day of Pentecost (Acts 2:1–4) at Caesarea in the family of Cornelius? (Acts 10:44–48). The Holy Spirit gives us all we need. If there is a change in manifestation, it is not because of a delineation of the Holy Spirit, but because of a change of need. The need today is different because we have the completed revelation of God's Holy Word, rather than a partial pouring out through various and sundry sermons.

Romans 5:6: "For while we were still helpless, at the right time Christ died for the ungodly." No person likes to think of him or herself as helpless, and no person is helpless in many respects. We are not helpless in the choosing of our own vocation, in the choosing of our mate, in the raising of our kids. We are not helpless in amassing financial independence, in our education, and in other pursuits. We are not helpless in seeking fame, if that is our goal. There is a lot in which we are not helpless. But in the restoring of a fractured relationship with God, in the being able to stand before Him in all purity, we are helpless. In regard to the eradication of the effect of sin, we are helpless. Sadly, the effect of sin is a separation from God. John 3:16 states, "For God so loved the world that He gave His only begotten Son…" There can be a loss of identity in that. We think of "the world" so much as a huge conglomerate, and we're just one little speck of nothing within that conglomerate. Many times when we say "the world," we lose personal identity with it. In John 3:16, if you take out "the world" and replace it with your name, then it becomes personal and really hits home.

In Romans 5:6 it says that "…at the right time Christ died for the ungodly." The right time… Galatians 4:4 uses the phrase "when the fullness of the time came." Galatians 4:4–6 says, "But when the fullness of the time came, God sent forth His Son, born of a woman, born under the Law, so that He might redeem those who were under the Law, that we might receive the adoption as sons. Because you are sons, God has sent forth the Spirit of His Son into our hearts, crying, 'Abba! Father!'" "The fullness of the time" is in reference to the time in which Jesus was born of a woman, born under the Law. That was the right time–for Europe, Northern Africa, and the Middle East never had been under one flag before that time, nor have they been since. The Far East wasn't involved, but the Roman Empire had spread as far north as England, as far south as Ethiopia, as far west as Portugal, and as far East as what would now be Afghanistan and all of the in-betweens. Rome built great roads into all of these areas, relying much upon the groundwork of Alexander the Great, who was a Greek and had spread his empire throughout the Middle East prior to the rise of Rome. It was a saying in the days of the Roman Empire that "all roads lead to Rome." The same roads that led the armies into the Roman Empire were the roads that brought the Christians back to Rome and throughout the Roman Empire.

The close of the book of Acts finds Paul preaching the Gospel unhindered in Rome. Throughout the Roman Empire, the Christians used the same roads that brought the invading hoards in and used them as highways for the Gospel. Early Christians did this not in armed conflict, but in a change of principle, in a change of philosophy, and in a change of heart. Let us fervently pray that as each terrorist nation topples because of armed might, there may be in its wake many, many who are carrying the Gospel to an un-reached society. By the very fact of liberty being brought to them, they will see the way of liberty, the way of peace, the way of prosperity, and the way that comes about through the power of the Gospel.

This next verse in chapter five is such a key verse, and it is one verse that is usually minimized here in this great thesis on grace. Romans 5:7 says, "For one will hardly die for a righteous man; though perhaps for the good man someone would dare even to die." If there is a criminal on death row, getting ready the following day to be put into the gas chamber, how many volunteers would come forth to change places with this guy? Yet, that is exactly what happened at the crucifixion of Christ when He took the place of Barabbas. Do you see the beautiful parallel and analogy of the glorious grace of God? Now, for a righteous man somebody might dare to die. You might be able to go to that criminal on death row and say, "Hey, wait a minute. We've got a Governor here in this state, but he has a couple of bad kidneys and the same type of blood as yours. Boy, you can save this macho man. Why go to the gas chamber and waste all of that? Let us transplant your kidneys to him since you are going to die anyway." For a good man someone might even dare to die, maybe. Maybe you can persuade him. But he might say, "Oh, well now, wait a minute. If this Governor is that macho and that great, he might give me a reprieve at the 11th hour. I don't think I am going to die for him. I am going to hang on to that one hope." Maybe, maybe you can persuade someone to give his life for a good man. But it wasn't for good people that Jesus died. It wasn't for the righteous, for there were none.

Chapter five continues (Romans 5:8), "But God demonstrates His own love toward us, in that while we were yet sinners, Christ died for us." This is not a good man dying for one not so good. This is God in the flesh. This is the passion of the cross. It wasn't the physical beating that caused Him to cry out in the great Garden of Gethsemane, "…remove this cup pass from me…" Mark 14:36. Rather, it was the beating that He knew was coming spiritually and emotionally, that separation from the Father. Jesus' love was manifested by His yielding completely to the will of God, which drove Him to the cross in order that He might take the penalty for our transgressions. Oh, the marvelous, wonderful grace of God! There is no composed song, no matter how beautiful, that can depict it, no golden oratorical tones that can properly articulate it. That God would be so merciful is above all that we can think, dream, or ask. That He would promise us a place in paradise if we call upon His name, in our dying condition, is incredible. What a climactic scene there is at the cross! The humans that orchestrated the crucifixion thought they had defeated this "King of the Jews," but God transformed defeat into this great, triumphant victory that we have in the death and resurrection of Jesus Christ.

Romans 5:9: "Much more then, having now been justified by His blood, we shall be saved from the wrath of God through Him." This verse is staggering. For the wrath of God is going to be poured out upon sin. Those who are caught within sin's grip will taste of that wrath. Those who voluntarily submit by faith to the grace of God will escape that wrath.

Romans 5:10: "For if while we were enemies we were reconciled to God through the death of His Son, much more, having been reconciled, we shall be saved by His life." Wait a minute; it says that He died for us, and now it says here that we are going to be saved by His life. That is because Easter came, bringing victory over death. He did not taste of His own death—remember, death was not in Him—but He tasted of ours. His life is greater than our sin, and He lives. So, as in the words of that old chorus 'He Lives,' "You ask me how I know He lives, He lives within my heart." But it is not just within our heart that He lives; He lives within countless millions of hearts. He is at the right hand of God, interceding right now on behalf of all who walk by faith (Romans 8:34).

Romans 5:11: "And not only this, but we also exult in God through our Lord Jesus Christ, through whom we have now received the reconciliation." Much more—oh, there is so much more to life in Christ!

QUESTIONS AND DISCUSSION FOR
GOD'S RIGHTEOUSNESS IS A GIFT OF GRACE

1. Faith brings _____ which brings _____. (See verse 1.)

2. Faith is our _____ to _____. (See verse 2.)

3. Name the parts that make up the circle of hope. (See verses 3–5.)

4. The power behind hope is the _____ of the _____. (See verse 5.)

5. What did God do when we were helpless? (See verse 6.)

6. When and how did God demonstrate His love for us? (See verse 8.)

7. What is almost impossible for one person to do for another? (See verse 7.)

8. For a righteous man someone might dare to _____. (See verse 7.)

9. Christ died for _____. (See verse 6.)

10. In spite of being enemies, we were _____ through the _____
   _____. (See verse 10.)

One Man's Righteousness Greater Than One Man's Sin

Romans 5:12–21

Now, let's go to an analogy—an analogy between Adam, the cause of all the chaos, and Jesus, the cure for all the chaos.

Romans 5:12 says, "Therefore, just as through one man sin entered into the world, and death through sin, and so death spread to all men, because all sinned…" One man, induced by Satan and then succumbing to Satan, sinned and thus sin entered the world. Same story today, sin same characters as far as the source, different characters as far as the response; however, it is the same response regardless of characters.

The third chapter of Genesis tells of the sin, the warning, and the consequences. One law existed—don't do it. One law was violated—they did it. The consequences—"thou shall surely die"— and God is true to His word. If He were not true to His word, He would not be a just God. If He was not just, He would be without His holiness. So man died in two ways. Initially that death was a spiritual death. He no longer walked and talked with God in the cool of the evening, and he was removed from the intimate presence of God. That garden is not seen reclaimed again by man until the 22nd chapter of Revelation. The end of the Bible circles about and brings man back to where he was at the beginning. The whole circle of human history is summed up in the person of Jesus and our re-acquaintance with Him. Not only was there spiritual death, but also the time clock for physical life began to tick. The Scriptures are silent on this, so I can only offer you an opinion. I don't know how many years, millions or billions, or days or weeks Adam and Eve were in the garden prior to their sin. But the time clock for aging began with the decay of the body, which was a result of physical death, the second way man died because of his sin. Spiritual death, physical death, and the days of man began to be counted when man began to age.

Although it is not generally highly thought of in evangelical circles, I am more comfortable with all of the ramifications of science and all of the ramifications of theology in the understanding that time began to tick when man was removed from the garden so that they could not live forever in their sin. The reason the Tree of Life was put into the garden was so that they could eat of that tree and live forever with God in the garden. But when they ate of the forbidden Tree of the Knowledge of Good and Evil, they were barred from the garden so that they could no longer eat of the Tree of Life and live forever in their sin. Their banishment was a great work of grace. This grace is seen in Jesus who never ate from the Tree of the Knowledge of Good and Evil, even though He was tempted in every way as we are (Hebrews 4:15).

So death, both spiritual and physical, spread to all men. Now inherent within man was a seed that had experienced sin; hence a seed of death spread to all men through Adam. The very second that you were conceived, it was predestined that you would die—not necessarily the manner or time, but the fact. The fact is that each and every one of us will have a memorial service held on our behalf. Death spread to all mankind. There is a separation from God so that we experience the same two types of death that Adam did.

Romans 5:13: "…for until the Law sin was in the world, but sin is not imputed when there is no law." Now we need to go back to Romans 2:12–16 to begin to refresh our memory as to how there is the imputing of sin without the Law. Romans 2:12 says, "For all who have sinned without the Law will also perish without the Law and all who have sinned under the Law will be judged by the Law." Oh, that is not very encouraging. Romans 2:13–16 continues, "for it is not the hearers of the Law who are just before God, but the doers of the Law will be justified. For when Gentiles who do not have the Law do instinctively the things of the Law, these, not having the Law, are a law to themselves, in that they show the work of the Law written in their hearts, their conscience bearing witness and their thoughts alternately accusing or else defending themselves, on the day when, according to my gospel, God will judge the secrets of men through Christ Jesus."

So, according to the above verses, to say, "Before the Law or outside of the Law we are not to be held guilty," is false. Or if you say, "If I just live according to the Ten Commandments I will be alright…" OK, I grant a person that. Let us take a test: read over the Ten Commandments, Exodus 20:1-17, and if you get over 20%, pat yourself on the back. There are probably only two that we can say we have held to. There are those who can say, "I have not committed adultery, and I didn't commit murder." We must not pass judgment on those who cannot reach to 20%. If you scored 20%, fantastic. I have had lots of grades, and as a teacher I've given out a few grades. I never passed anybody with 20%, and I never got a passing grade with 20%. Although I wasn't much higher than that when my Greek professor said, "Ted, you are saved by grace and not by works." Thank God for grace.

GOD'S RIGHTEOUSNESS IS A GIFT OF GRACE

The Law is imputed by our conscience when we do instinctively the things of the Law. In the most barbaric, heathenish, primitive societies there is still this instinctive principle regarding stealing, sexual impropriety, etc.—although in many barbaric societies it is broadened. For example, in Africa you can have multiple wives. That is the dumbest law I have ever heard of. It is difficult to get along with one let alone multiple wives. But there is a standard that every society establishes instinctively, because we are created in the image of God and have embedded within us that divine spark. We innately create a code of human behavior.

Romans 5:14 continues, "Nevertheless death reigned from Adam until Moses, even over those who had not sinned in the likeness of the offense of Adam, who is a type of Him who was to come." Let's look at the result of transgression. Adam's offense was a direct violation to a direct command. Now, just because there is not a direct command, that does not negate the fact that we have sinned. So our sin is not in the likeness of Adam's sin "…who is a type…" or a shadow or a figure "…of Him who was to come."

One of the most fascinating courses I took, and perhaps the course that had the greatest effect upon my theology and my own personal life, was a course in Bible College called "Typology." It was taught by a great, great scholar of the Old Testament, a tremendous man, V.K. Allison. I was as green as a gourd. I'd only been a Christian for about 18 months, and I didn't know up from down. If they told me it was in 2nd Habakkuk, I would search all over for that book. My first semester in Bible College, I ended up in a third year class on Typology. It was one of the hardest yet one of the most fascinating classes I have ever taken. Typology takes all of the shadows, all of the types, of the Messiah that are given in the Old Testament and parallels them to the New Testament. One of the first types would be Adam as a type of Christ. The New Testament scripture that we used after thoroughly studying what Adam did was in Romans 5:12 and following. I am going to share with you some of the concepts that were reaped in those early days.

Romans 5:15: "But the free gift is not like the transgression…" Here we have a type which is parallel, and yet we start out with this type noting differences. Verse 15 continues, "…For if by the transgression of the one the many died, …" That sure is the truth. Physically we are all predestined to die, and spiritually we are also predestined to die if we remain in our sin, that is, aloof from God. But here is where the difference comes. The second part of that duel death can be averted because of God's grace. Let's see how that works out (verse 15): "…much more did the grace of God and the gift by the grace of the one Man, Jesus Christ, abound to the many." Notice two quick points. One, the universality of physical and spiritual death was brought about by Adam. Two, the universality of the possibility of spiritual death is being eradicated by Christ. I say the possibility because there has to be a reaction to that act of grace before grace can take effect. That reaction is faith. With faith, the assurance of the universality of that cleansing from sin is as sure as our physical death by its occurrence.

"The gift is not like that which came through the one who sinned; for on the one hand the judgment arose from one transgression resulting in condemnation, but on the other hand the free gift arose from many transgressions being forgiven, resulting in justification. Or if by the transgression of the one, death reigned through the one, much more those who receive the abundance of grace and of the gift of righteousness will reign in life through the One, Jesus Christ" (Romans 5:16–17). So Jesus Christ takes the place on the throne regarding life and death. The death that remains is physical, for that was our inception or conception, whichever you prefer. The gift of spiritual life is also by conception or inception. Jesus spoke about this in John 3:3–5: "Jesus answered and said to him, 'Truly, truly, I say to you, unless one is born again he cannot see the kingdom of God.' Nicodemus said to Him, 'How can a man be born when he is old? He cannot enter a second time into his mother's womb and be born, can he?' Jesus answered, 'Truly, truly, I say to you, unless one is born of water and the Spirit he cannot enter into the kingdom of God.'" There is a change of verb from "see" in John 3:3 to "enter" in John 3:5. It was the Spirit of God that quickened life into Adam—God breathed into man the breath of life. It was the Spirit of God that brought conformity out of non-conformity, going clear back to Genesis 1:2. It was the Spirit of God that conceived within Mary that babe who would be born the Son of God (Luke 2:35). Hence, in that conception, there is no element of sin. For the seed by which He was conceived was that of the Holy Spirit, not of the sin-infested seed of mankind. This same Holy Spirit that has been the author and inducer and promoter and the inception of life all the way through, is that same Holy Spirit that is a gift to you and is the means for the obtaining of that gift. And that is done by faith.

The last four verses in Romans 5, verses 18–21, are a summation of not only this chapter but also of all the previous chapters. These verses tie it all together. Romans 5:18 says, "So then as through one transgression there resulted condemnation to all men, even so through one act of righteousness there resulted justification of life to all men." The fact that all have sinned is evident in Romans 1:18–3:20. Then the Righteousness of God appears, and we are justified rather than condemned. As condemnation is to all mankind, so justification is available to all mankind. Romans 5:19 states, "For as through the one man's disobedience the many were made sinners, even so through the obedience of the One the many will be made righteous." Disobedience makes us sinners. Obedience leads us to righteousness. Adam is the one who ushered in disobedience. Jesus is the one who ushered in righteousness. Jesus overrides the power of sin (Romans 1:15–16). This is the message we are privileged to proclaim.

"And the Law came in that the transgression might increase; but where sin increased, grace abounded all the more…" (Romans 5:20). Not so much was there an increase in the number of sins committed, but there was a greater knowledge of what constitutes sin. Apart from the Law, what was counted as sin was determined by conscience (Romans 2:12–16). One person's conscience is not the same as another person's in all things. There was no consistent norm to gauge what was sin. Sin runs rampant without law (Genesis 6:5–6; 19). With the giving of the Law, God established a definitive knowledge of what constitutes sin. With this increased knowledge, there was and is an increased knowledge of sin. And remember, death's stinging smite is the result of sin. But the blessed assurance we have in Jesus is that His grace is greater than our sin. Romans 5:21: "…so that, as sin reigned in death, even so grace might reign through righteousness to eternal life through Jesus Christ our Lord."

QUESTIONS AND DISCUSSION FOR ONE MAN'S RIGHTEOUSNESS GREATER THAN ONE MAN'S SIN.

1. Where there is no law there is no _____ ; where there is law there is _____. (See verses 13 and 20.)

2. Why was there death before Moses? (See verse 14.)

3. In Verse 14, what is a "type"?

4. Discuss how the righteousness of Jesus can be as universal in its effect of bringing life as was the sin of Adam in bringing death.

5. Discuss why grace is greater than sin.

Chapter 6

The Greatness of Sin Does Not Increase the Greatness of Grace

Romans 6:1–23

Introduction

WE REALIZE THAT even though one person introduced sin and death, sin and death came unto all of mankind. Likewise, through one person righteousness was introduced, which is also available to all mankind. That which has been formed from the dust of the earth returns to dust and that which has been created or breathed or spirited into man returns to the Creator (Ecclesiastes 12:6–7). Salvation has been revealed to us in the person of Jesus. It transcends the Law, including both those under the Law and those outside of the Law, for all are in desperate need of grace. This great righteousness can be obtained by faith. There is a work of faith that leads us to the grace of God. Don't you want to get all of this grace that you can? Man, pour it on, fill my cup, let it run over, let it go down to the saucer, let the saucer run over, let it spoil the tablecloth, make it so wet that it drips on the floor. Oh, give us grace. As they used to say in the South: "I'm sitting under the spout where the Glory comes out." God keeps pouring out His grace time after time after time; that is the way it is with God. His grace covers all of our sins; doesn't that mean the greatest sinners receive the greatest amount of grace? Probably! Yes! So if I want more grace, then should I delve deeper into sin in order to receive more grace? What do you think of that? Hear Paul's response and his reasons for why this type of sordid thinking is erroneous. Chapter six opens with a similar question. Let's see what Paul has to say.

Justification Brings Freedom from Sin's Power

Romans 6:1–11

Romans 6:1–2: "What shall we say then? Are we to continue in sin so that grace may increase? May it never be!" Paul's answer to our question is short and sweet. In the King James Version this reads, "God forbid." I like that translation the best. Verse 2 continues, "How shall we who died to sin still live in it?" Now we are ready for the next question: if you died to sin, why do you keep living in it? So we must determine what constitutes being dead to sin and what power or ability that being dead to sin releases.

Romans 6:3: "Or do you not know …" Don't you remember? Wasn't it ever brought to your attention? Don't you realize? Don't you get it? "…that all of us who have been baptized into Christ Jesus have been baptized into His death?" In other words, being baptized is more than becoming a member of an ecclesiastical organization. Being baptized is more than a symbol.

I just don't find the word "symbol" in conjunction with baptism in Scripture. The closest reference is found in 1 Peter 3:21. I don't know of any other Scripture that even makes an illusion to baptism as being symbolic. It says, "…after a true likeness or figure does now save you even baptism, not the washing away of the filth of the flesh, but the interrogation or the answering of a good conscience toward God through the resurrection of Jesus." That "figure" relates back to the physical cleansing of the earth during the days of Noah. So if we go back three or four verses in 1 Peter 3, we see that the symbolism relates to Noah and the cleansing of the flood—how he was saved by the water. Then Peter points out that baptism is not a bath tub; it is not a physical cleansing. It is a cleansing or the answering of a good conscience, which deals with the heart, and can only be rectified through the resurrection and our associating with the resurrection of Jesus Christ.

Does that mean that we actually go back to the cross and that we are strapped on the cross with Him? What strapped Him on the cross? It was our own sin. We were there. That is the whole gist of this thing. We were baptized into His death. It isn't that we go back; it is that the effect of the death of Christ, the purpose of the death of Christ, comes forward and meets us where we are. Once this happens, we are in a repentant, faithful, and obedient attitude, crowning Him as the Lord of our life. We then are enjoined in the whole predetermined process of salvation. Is that enjoining real or is it symbolic? I hope it is really real in our lives and hearts—that we know in whom we have believed, we know in whom we have confidence, we know in whom we trust, and that knowledge is without any doubt because we have shared in His death.

Romans 6:4 says, "Therefore we have been buried with Him through baptism into death…" I have heard this verse used more often to substantiate immersion over sprinkling, and I think that is such a discredit to the depth of this verse. In the first place, the very term "baptism" is not an English word. It is a transliteration, the taking of a Greek word and putting an English ending on that Greek word. The definition of the word "baptism," from a secular and scholarly standpoint, apart from any religious overtones, means to plunge, submerge, immerse. So we don't need to borrow this being buried with Christ to prove immersion over sprinkling. The word itself has the foundation within it to demonstrate that. What then is the intent? "…we have been buried with Him through baptism into death…" We have been overwhelmed; we have been immersed in the death of Christ. We have been surrounded in the death of Christ, and the death of Christ is the one and only sacrifice that can ever be made for the forgiveness of our sins. So we were buried with Him, overwhelmed by His death, satisfied by His death, completely covered by His death, and all of our sin has been forgiven.

Verse 4 continues, "…so that as Christ was raised from the dead through the glory of the Father…" This is starting to get good! Up from the grave He arose! Today, and on each Easter Sunday morning, this proclamation starts out in the South Pacific Islands and winds up in Hawaii, spreading all the way around the world proclaiming the living Christ, the risen Christ. "…So we too might walk in newness of life." Tie this back to John 3:3–5, where Jesus, talking with Nicodemus, said you have to be born again or you cannot see the kingdom of God. How is this done? It is done by the water and the Spirit, in order to enter the kingdom of heaven. So we find that we have a new life—same nose, same chin, same girth, but the newness is in the head and in the emotions, the part that really makes us what we are. While we are identified by our bodies, we are known by what we think and how we feel, and that is where the new life takes place.

Romans 6:5: "For if we have become united with Him in the likeness of His death…" (I like this next word) "…certainly we shall also be in the likeness of His Resurrection…" The bonus comes in this verse. We usually look at this verse prophetically or futuristically. When do we become a joint heir with Christ—following our demise physically or following our being crucified with Christ? So when do we become this new creature? If we wrestle with this from a physical standpoint, we are going to come to the only sound conclusion. This likeness in His resurrection is going to be after our demise. So let's think about our being a new creature in Christ in a spiritual context—that is, new in minds, new in goals, new in ambitions, new in attitudes, and new in desires. All of this comprises the new man in Christ, and hence, it is spiritual. Look at it in a spiritual context. It excludes the things we did that we are not continuing to do now and the life we lived that we are not living now. In a more positive way, the life that we are living in Christ can only be accomplished as we share in the power of His resurrection. This new life is ours! Let us not demean the beauty of a Christian life. I think, and this is purely an opinion, that this passage has reference to our walk with Christ. This passage has to do with our being a raised person in our intellect, in our emotions, and hence, in our physical stand. Colossians 2:12 states, "…having been buried with Him in baptism, in which you were also raised up with Him through faith in the working of God, who raised Him from the dead." 2 Corinthians 5:17 substantiates our relationship with Christ and takes it a step further in saying that we are a new creature in Him.

Romans 6:6: "…knowing this, that our old self was crucified with Him …" Let's check Galatians 2:20, which says, "I have been crucified with Christ; and it is no longer I who live, but Christ lives in me; and the life which I now live in the flesh I live by faith in the Son of God, who loved me and gave Himself up for me." First, it requires the acceptance of the lordship of Jesus in order that we might attain to the salvation that He offers. And second, in this acceptance of the lordship of Jesus, the old self was crucified with Him. Verse 6 continues, "… that our body of sin might be done away with, so that we would no longer be slaves to sin…"

Romans 6:7: "…for he who has died is freed from sin." A great statement is made in this verse—perhaps one of the greatest statements in the whole sixth chapter and one that is often overlooked. The consequences (the penalty) of sin have been paid, the debt has been removed, and we are freed from sin. Does that mean I'll never sin again? First John 1:9–10 says, "If we confess our sins, He is faithful and righteous to forgive us our sins and to cleanse us from all unrighteousness. If we say that we have not sinned, we make Him a liar and His word is not in us." For the person who practices sin, who continues in sin habitually, and who, with premeditation (knowingly) is slapping God in the face, as long as that person is in that unrepentant condition, the blood of Christ that once covered him or her, the spirit that once sealed him or her, is no longer in effect. But it is not the aberration of sinning; it is the continual practice of sinning (Hebrews 10:26–31). What got us into Christ, our faith, must continue for us to remain in Him.

Romans 6:8: "Now if we have died with Christ, we believe that we shall also live with Him…" That belief is predicated upon His resurrection. If we died with Him, we believe that we will be raised with Him. If He is the risen and living Christ, then we live with Him. It is all interwoven here, and Paul is just attacking it from every direction that he can in order to get us to appreciate what Christ is doing in such a dramatic way. Romans 6:9: "…knowing that Christ, having been raised from the dead, is never to die again; death no longer is master over Him." Physically, He has already died; that is in the past, but He was raised again. He will never die, so His relationship with God is unbroken. Time cannot measure it. Physically, we might as well make an appointment with the undertaker, because the very instant in which we were conceived, death was predetermined. The seed that caused conception (thanks, Adam) insured that you would die, because in that seed was inherent death. So every person, physically, is going to die. But our physical demise will be a release, as was Jesus' physical demise, to have a greater experience with Almighty God. This is just like Christ did by letting go of His spiritual life in order to become fashioned as we are and to become obedient even unto death. God highly exalted Him, and if we are joint heirs with Jesus, we then shall be highly exalted at the termination of our journey here on earth. Verse 10 says, "For the death that He died, He died to sin once for all; but the life that He lives, He lives to God." The sacrifice that Jesus made at Calvary is sufficient for all mankind for all the ages. The life that Jesus gives us is as endless as God, for it is a life given to God. Oh, the mighty blessings that are ours when we become joined with Jesus in the likeness of His death, burial, and resurrection!

"Even so consider yourselves to be dead to sin, but alive to God in Christ Jesus" (Romans 6:11). Consider that carefully. Give it a lot of thought. Bask in its beauty.

QUESTIONS AND DISCUSSION FOR JUSTIFICATION BRINGS FREEDOM FROM SIN'S POWER

1. What is the question? (See verse 1.)

2. What roll does our Baptism have in the answer to the question? (Hebrews 10:26–29; 1 John 2:1–5).

3. Likeness of His _____ we will be in the likeness of His _____ _____. (See verse 5.)

4. We walk in _____ newness of _____. (See verse 4.)

5. We are freed _____. (See verse 7.)

6. Our union with Jesus brings what promises? _____. (See verse 8.)

7. Consider ourselves as dead to _____ and alive to _____. (See verse 11.)

8. Discuss if Baptism is symbolic or real to its object.

The End of the Reign of Sin

Romans 6:12–23

Romans 6:12: "Therefore do not let..." I've got the word "let" underlined in my Bible. This word "let" infers that we have a choice. Before we had no choice, because we were slaves to a master who was greater than we were; and even though we desired to do that which was good, we did not perform accordingly. We had a sickness, a sin sickness, but in Christ Jesus we do not have to allow ourselves to remain ill. Since we have been joined in the death, burial, resurrection, and life of Jesus, it is a part of us. Sure, you will have your garden of Gethsemane; sure, you will cry out; sure, you will look for another way—but there is also that yielding to the will of God. And as that yielding to the will of God increases, regardless of what we ingest or what practices we may have been involved in, we don't need to "let" those things control our lives. Verse 12 continues, "…do not let sin reign in your mortal body so that you obey its lusts…" Oh, the power Jesus had when He broke the chains of sin and rose from the dead! Free, free at last, when He allowed us to be joined with Him in the likeness of His resurrection.

Romans 6:13: "…and do not go on presenting the members of your body to sin as instruments of unrighteousness…" Let us look again at Romans 6:1, which says, "What shall we say then, are we to continue in sin that grace may increase?" Romans 6:13 folds back to that opening question and addresses it. It says, don't do it. We don't need to! Romans 6:13: "…but present yourselves to God as those alive from the dead and your members as instruments of righteousness to God." This folds all the way back to the theme of the book: "for therein is revealed the righteousness of God from faith unto faith that is through the Gospel the power of salvation" (Romans 1:16–17, paraphrased). The demonstrating of that righteousness is seen in Romans 3:20–21, and now we come right back to it. We are instruments or tools of righteousness, and so our bodies are now performing activities that are relying upon that righteousness.

Romans 6:14 continues the thought: "For sin shall not be master over you…" Before, we could not stop ourselves from allowing or letting our sin nature control us, but now we have something else, as verse 14 concludes, "…for you are not under law but under grace." The Law primarily deals with the deeds of the flesh and does not sufficiently attack the source of those deeds, the heart and mind. Within the Law, the greatest commandment of all was to love the Lord your God with all of your heart (Matthew 22:34–40). It dealt with the emotions. But those emotions are imperfect, and the Law imputed that imperfection and demanded justice for its violation, and hence, death came. But under grace there is the fulfillment of the Law, not the obliteration of it. In that fulfillment of the Law, then, when we assume God's grace for us, we are freed from the penalty of that Law.

Romans 6:15: "What then? Shall we sin because we are not under law but under grace? May it never be!" That is the same question, in principle, that was asked in the first verse. Now Paul is going to attack that same question in a different manner. Verse 16: "Do you not know that when you present yourselves to someone as slaves for obedience, you are slaves of the one whom you obey, either of sin resulting in death, or of obedience resulting in righteousness?" What more can God do than what He has done? I think that was the great question that Jesus asked at Gethsemane. What more could He do? So in this verse Paul is, in essence, saying that the ball is in your court. You can choose the life that leads to heartache and tears, or you can choose a life that brings with it stability, new goals, new motives, new outlets, and a new future.

THE GREATNESS OF SIN DOES NOT INCREASE THE GREATNESS OF GRACE

Romans 6:17: "But thanks be to God that though you were slaves of sin, you became obedient from the heart to that form of teaching to which you were committed…" Our obedience to the will of God starts in our spiritual dimension. Faith comes by hearing the Word of God. The Bible is the witness given to us regarding Christ. Once that witness has been brought to us, we have the opportunity of rejecting it, saying, "Wait a minute, I want to hear some more," or just accepting it by faith. Once we have accepted that witness, our emotions are stirred, so we become physically obedient to whatever command God may make. Now it is not a matter of debate, it is a matter of faith. It is not a matter of works, it is a matter of following our heart in the decision we make to walk in the pathways of Christ. Verse 18 begins, "…and having been freed from sin…" Ah, I love it! Freed from slavery, freed from an involuntary subjection to that from which we could not in our own power free ourselves, "and having been freed from sin, you became slaves of righteousness." We are free to become "slaves of righteousness." This is a voluntary result of the heart action that we take. We are not *compelled* by God, we are *entreated* by God. In that entreating we respond to the call of love rather than the harsh voice of a forced taskmaster of sin.

Romans 6:19: "I am speaking in human terms because of the weakness of your flesh. For just as you presented your members as slaves to impurity and to lawlessness, resulting in further lawlessness, so now present your members as slaves to righteousness, resulting in sanctification." I love that word "sanctification." It means to set apart for a holy use—sanctified. Does it take an additional work other than our being cleansed by the blood of Christ? What other additional work could even begin to compare to the work He did for us upon Calvary? To hold to that proposition of works is a demeaning of the shedding of Christ's blood.

Romans 6:20–21: "For when you were slaves of sin, you were free in regard to righteousness. Therefore what benefit were you then deriving from the things of which you are now ashamed? For the outcome of those things is death." What benefit does the world really give to you? Wealth can be taken by a fire, earthquake, hurricane, or flood; so then, where are you? Fame is so fleeting. How many of you remember who sang with Jeannette McDonald? Ask a teenager today, and he or she will say, "Who in the world is Jeannette McDonald?" Never mind who she sang with. Fame feels so good at the time, but it is gone in a whisper. And what are the benefits and the outcome of our being freed from sin? "But now having been freed from sin and enslaved to God, you derive your benefit, resulting in sanctification, and the outcome, eternal life. For the wages of sin is death, but the free gift of God is eternal life in Christ Jesus our Lord" (Romans 6:22–23).

QUESTIONS AND DISCUSSION FOR THE END OF THE REIGN OF SIN

1. Do not let _____ (1Cor.15:55–56).

2. Present yourselves to _____. (See verse 13.)

3. Why will sin not master us? _____. (See verse 14.)

4. What are the two masters we can present ourselves to? _____ (See verse 16.)

5. What is the benefit of serving sin? _____ (See verse 21.)

6. What is the benefit in our enslavement to God? _____. (See verse 22.)

7. The contrast between the wage and the free gift is _____ (See verse 23.)

Chapter 7

From A Covenant that Brought Death to a Covenant that Brings Life

Romans 7:1–25

Introduction

THE BIBLE WAS not written in chapters and verses. For instance, the book of Romans was written like we would write a letter to someone. But centuries later, for the sake of discovering particular passages and making it easier to study, it was divided into chapters and verses. Sometimes books of the Bible have been divided into chapters very astutely, and sometimes you wonder why in the world there is a new chapter.

In our thinking, a chapter usually indicates a change in character or direction, or it is a definite, progressive step that is a building block in a book. But this is not always so in the Bible. Sometimes if we approach a new chapter divorced from the previous chapter, we are going to draw all kinds of conclusions that might be erroneous. This is the case in the seventh chapter of the book of Romans. It is a continuation of the sixth chapter as far as thought, content, and principle are concerned.

We have become a part of the consequences of sin, which results in a fractured relationship with God in this earthly life. We desperately need to have that relationship mended. That fractured relationship results in an immediate death, which is a separation from God, for we are dead in our trespasses and sin. Sin has a long-range spiritual consequence—the eternal separation from God. No matter if you take hell figuratively or literally, the bottom line is the same. It is going to be dark, it is going to be fiery, and it is going to be without any foundation. There are at least three characteristics of hell in the New Testament: the outer darkness (Matthew 25:20), the lake of fire (Revelation 20:14), and the bottomless pit (Revelation 20:9), Hell must be as meaningful to our psyche, our spirit, our personality, and our character as is heaven.

To be freed from the slavery of sin (and ultimately from hell), we enter into voluntary servitude to God through Jesus Christ. We are motivated to do this because of the greatness of God's grace. We choose Him to be the Landlord of this body of clay, and thus, He controls the mind and the heart that is vested in this body. The action of the body responds to the mind and the heart.

Jurisdiction of the Law

Romans 7:1–6

The last chapter opened with a question: "What shall we say then, are we to continue in sin that grace may increase?" (Romans 6:1). As we begin to look at chapter seven, notice that it operates in almost the same manner, except it is going to hone in on the slavery that has the sting of the Law. It is going to deal with the fact that we are freed from the Law's sting.

Romans 7:1 begins, "Or do you not know, brethren (for I am speaking to those who know the law), that the law has jurisdiction over a person as long as he lives?" Now he draws an illustration of marriage in verse 2: "For the married woman is bound by law to her husband while he is living; but if her husband dies, she is released from the law concerning the husband." That contract has been finished, the covenant has been completed. The marriage covenant is like the covenant, the contract that God had made with the people who were under the Law. They, the people, were under the Law as long as that covenant remained. But once that contract was completed or fulfilled, they were freed from the obligations and privileges of the Law. In the marriage covenant, when a woman becomes a widow she has an opportunity, if she desires, to seek another lover. When we can see what Jesus, the magnificent lover of our lives, hearts, and souls, did for us, we ought to just jump at the opportunity to willingly accept His lordship and to voluntarily be in servitude to Him.

Many times this passage of Scripture is used either as an argument for or against divorce. I think that even introducing that topic in relation to this particular passage is doing a great, great injustice. Rather than discussing divorce, this is illustrating the fact that we become dead to the Law when we become alive in Christ. We are no longer under the demands and under the consequences of the violation of that Law. The demands and the consequences for our violation of the law were met by Jesus at the cross, and we are now free to willingly and longingly join ourselves to Him.

Romans 7:3: "So then, if while her husband is living she is joined to another man, she shall be called an adulteress; but if her husband dies, she is free from the law, so that she is not an adulteress though she is joined to another man." Oh, Jews, he was pleading here. Do not feel as though you are committing adultery to God by the violation and the departure from the Law, for the Law is dead. The principles of the Law are maintained in an era of grace, and the procedures of the Law have been superseded in order to fulfill the complete principles of the Law, which was done through the person of Christ. This observation plays a major role in our appreciation of the Old Testament and its role in bringing us into this New Covenant in Christ.

I was teaching along these lines one evening, and there was a doctor in the audience. He was a fine man, was retired, and came from a background where there is a great intermixing of the Law and of grace. His family worshipped on Saturday.

Do we observe the Sabbath? Absolutely we do. Our Sabbath is not a particular day but a life of rest. It is not a specific day of worship, it is our rest in Jesus (Matt. 11:28, Col. 2:16–19, Heb. 4:10–11).

An example of freedom from the Law comes to mind. We have a minister across the street from us who preaches for this particular fellowship. One day he was complaining to me. He observed, "You know, we are supposed to rest on the Sabbath, and on the Sabbath I work harder than any other day."

I scratched my head and said, "Well, gee, then do you feel as though you are violating the Sabbath?"

He continued, "Oh, well, ah, no!"

I then commented, "Oh, well, that is interesting." I then saw him one Saturday, and he was in his grubbies. I have never seen him in his grubbies on Saturday. They were going to have a big rally down at the convention center in town and somebody came in the night before and stole all their computers and so he had to hurry home and grab his computer and run it down there. I said, "Well, that's OK. You know, I think this qualifies as an 'ox in the ditch' (Luke 14:5). Don't you?"

He turned and smiled at me and said, "Yeah, it sure does."

The point is that our Sabbath is in our rest in Christ. We entered our Sabbath when we entered into the death, burial, and resurrection relationship with God. We then rest from the burden and the consequence of sin. Our Sabbath is our relationship with God. This is Jesus' invitation when He says in Matthew 11:28, "Come to Me all who are weary and heavy-laden and I will give you rest." This rest is for our soul, spirit, heart, and mind. With this understanding, the fourth chapter of Hebrews really comes alive, and Colossians 2:16–19 makes really good sense.

Let's continue with Romans 7:4: "Therefore, my brethren, you also were (past tense) made to die to the Law through the body of Christ, that you might be joined to another, to Him who was raised from the dead, in order that we might bear fruit for God." So here we are in this new relationship with a new suitor, a new lover of our souls, who never fails and is filled with grace.

Romans 7:5: "For while we were in the flesh, the sinful passions, which were aroused by the Law, were at work in the members of our body to bear fruit for death." We couldn't control it. How many of you knew what was right and didn't do it? How many of you knew what was wrong and you did it? I am really dating myself, but do you remember the old radio program called "Red Skelton"? He would play this naughty little boy. He would say, "If I doed it, I get a whippen." Then there was this pause. He would go on to say, "I doed it!" He knew the consequences, but he did it anyway. That is our life outside of Christ. We know that the consequences are going to come, but we see the glitter, the appeal, and the romance of the moment. That overrides our judgment so that we become slaves to those consequences.

Romans 7:6: "But now we have been released from the Law ..." I've underlined that sixth verse in my Bible; it is so important. Verse 6 continues, "... having died to that by which we were bound, so that we serve in newness of the Spirit and not in oldness of the letter." The capital "S" in "Spirit" is referring to a divine Spirit, the Spirit of God, the Spirit of Holiness, or the Holy Spirit.

QUESTIONS AND DISCUSSION FOR JURISDICTION OF THE LAW

1. This chapter is directed to the _____. (See verse 1.)

2. What is the main point of the illustration of husband and wife? (See verses 2–4.)

3. How does it apply to us and the Law? (See verses 4 and 6.)

4. What importance is given to the "body of Christ"? (See verse 4.)

5. The result is that we bear _____ for _____. (See verse 4.)

6. Serve in the newness of _____ not in the oldness of the _____. (See verse 6.)

The Law is not Sin; it is Holy and Spiritual

Romans 7:7–25

Romans 7:7: "What shall we say then? Is the Law sin? " No, no the Law is not sin. The Law pointed out what was sin. The Law was perfect, and that was the problem. The perfection of the Law and the imperfection of hearer or bearer of the Law were incompatible. If the Law is perfect and just, then a commensurate penalty for the violation of that Law must be maintained. If it is not maintained, then the Law becomes imperfect. So is the Law sinful? Verse 7 continues, "... May it never be! On the contrary, I would not have come to know sin except through the Law; for

FROM A COVENANT THAT BROUGHT DEATH
TO A COVENANT THAT BRINGS LIFE

I would not have known about coveting if the Law had not said, 'YOU SHALL NOT COVET.'"
We would have coveted and committed other sins freely, including murder, adultery, or lying.

The standards of the Law are elevated beginning in Matthew chapter five. Note comments
on this in Chapter 3, where this is discussed in detail.

Romans 7:8–10: "But sin, taking opportunity through the commandment, produced in me
coveting of every kind; for apart from the Law sin is dead. I was once alive apart from the Law;
but when the commandment came, sin became alive and I died; and this commandment, which
was to result in life, proved to result in death for me..." He is talking about his life outside of
grace, whether it be under the Law of Moses or under the Law of conscience. Romans 7:11–13:
"...for sin, taking an opportunity through the commandment, deceived me and through it
killed me. So then, the Law is holy, and the commandment is holy and righteous and good.
Therefore did that which is good become a cause of death for me? May it never be! Rather it
was sin..." The Law pointed out what is right and wrong, but it was the violation of the Law,
not the Law itself, that brought death.

Let me share a puny illustration (man, is this puny!): Let's say there is an intersection without
a stop sign, but the cross traffic is still pretty good. Since it doesn't have a stop sign, I could
just go right on through. I could go through at any speed. I wouldn't get a ticket for going fast
or going through...but I might get killed. On the other hand, if there were a stop sign, even if
there's no traffic coming, I'd have to stop; it's the law. It would be the same if there were a red
light and no traffic coming. I could sit and sit there and think that the thing must be stuck. I
could look around and think, *I am sure it is stuck.* I could creep across, and just about the time
I get into the middle of the intersection, the light could turn green, and I say, "Oh, well. I went
through while it was green anyway." But what I did would still be a violation of the law. And
the violation of the law, when caught, dictates a penalty appropriate to the crime committed.

Since God knows everything, sees everything, and understands the intents of our hearts as
well as the actions of our bodies, it is absolutely imperative that the Law becomes an instrument
of death. But is the Law death itself? Not at all; sin is. The Law became that instrument because
it pronounces the penalty for violation. We are the perpetrators, and hence, due the penalty
of that great, great crime. Romans 7:13–14: "... in order that it might be shown to be sin by
effecting my death through that which is good, that through the commandment sin would
become utterly sinful. For we know that the Law is spiritual, but I am of flesh, sold into bondage
to sin." This was Paul's life before he became a slave of Christ.

In the remainder of this chapter of Romans is an analogy between the life before we became
a Christian and the life that we now have in Christ. Let us not borrow the principle of that old
life and apply it to the victories that we have now. We must remember that the fight of those
under the Law was futile. It was a fight they could not win, but not so in our Christian life.
Our weaknesses are gone, washed away by the blood of Christ. An inner strength is ours by an

infusion of the Holy Spirit, which helps us to obey and be able to do all things through Christ who strengthens us (Phil 4:13). What a difference!

Romans 7:15–17: "For that which I am doing, I do not understand; for I am not practicing what I would like to do, but I am doing the very thing I hate. But if I do the very thing I do not want to do, I agree with the Law, confessing that the Law is good. So now, no longer am I the one doing it, but sin which dwells in me." Paul is talking about a life of compulsory slavery to sin, not a life of voluntary slavery to Jesus Christ. Verse 18: "For I know that nothing good dwells in me, that is, in my flesh; for the willing is present in me, but the doing of the good is not." Now, some good is done. It is very, very rare that a person is so totally depraved, is so reprobate in mind and thought that he or she is beyond redemption. That is an aberration to human behavior. Most people have some good impulses in them. Verse 19: "For the good that I want, I do not do, but I practice the very evil that I do not want." That was the situation under the Law. Verse 20: "But if I am doing the very thing I do not want, I am no longer the one doing it, but sin which dwells in me." Thus sin is the master of our lives. Verses 21–23 continue, "I find then the principle that evil is present in me, the one who wants to do good. For I joyfully concur with the law of God in the inner man, but I see a different law in the members of my body, waging war against the law of my mind and making me a prisoner of the law of sin which is in my members." He can only conclude in verse 24, "Wretched man that I am…" Then a beautiful question is asked (verse 24): "…Who will set me free from the body of this death?" The answer? We were set free from this torment and turmoil. Verse 25 says, "Thanks be to God through Jesus Christ our Lord! So then, on the one hand I myself with my mind am serving the law of God, but on the other, with my flesh the law of sin."

This dichotomy is in existence that the consequence for our sins was changed because the penalty for our sins was paid in the person of Jesus. That is good news! It is the reason why we should not continue in sin so that grace may abound. In continuing in sin, we make an affront against God, against the sacrifice that He paid, against the very atonement of His blood, against the Holy Spirit that sealed us, and against the walk that we have in a newness of life. This is spelled out in Hebrews 10:26–29 (all parentheses mine). Verse 26 states, "For if we go on sinning willfully (deliberately, knowingly, cunningly, without any remorse or repentance) after receiving the knowledge of the truth, there no longer remains a sacrifice for sins…" Whoa! What happened to the blood on the cross? Verses 27–29 continue, "…but a terrifying expectation of judgment, and *the fury of a fire which will consume the adversaries* (because we are outside the sacrifice). Anyone who has set aside the Law of Moses dies without mercy on the testimony of two or three witnesses (that is the Law). How much severer punishment do you think he will deserve who has trampled under foot the Son of God, and has regarded as unclean the blood of the covenant by which he was sanctified, and has insulted the Spirit of grace?" Notice the verb tense in all of this—who "has been sanctified," who "has been covered" by the blood of Christ. There is nothing, no outside pressure, no spiritual pressure that can separate us from the love of God. We are more than conquerors through Him. We will see this more as we study the eighth chapter of Romans.

The whole book of Romans is predicated upon the action of God and the reaction of man. The action of God is grace; the reaction of man is faith. As long as we maintain our faith in the Lord Jesus Christ, there is nothing that can separate us from the grace of God. But it takes faith to get to that position, and if faith is violated or broken, we no longer are believers or yield to the lordship of Jesus. We go back into the ways of the world that we were living in prior to our becoming cleansed by the blood of Christ. Note Hebrews 10:26–29. So are we once in grace always in grace? Yes, as long as we have our faith, absolutely. But when we willfully violate, surrendering our faith, taking that faith of the lordship of Jesus away, we put ourselves at risk. There may be circumstances that pressure us; we rationalize it in any way we can. But no matter how much rationalization we do, there exists great risk.

Is there any hope of restoration? Absolutely. God will deal with you exactly as He dealt with you before you became a Christian, and there can be a reinstatement. Does this mean that I need to be re-baptized? I don't know. I would not say so, and I would not demand it, because that would be an affront against the basic principle for our association with the death, burial, and resurrection in the first place. But it does certainly mean, if not publicly, at least privately, a reaffirmation and dedication of our faith and confidence in the Lordship of Jesus Christ. Then the effect of this will be that your life will be evidence of that recommitment. There is a distinct difference between the continued practice of the same sin and the sin which is an aberration of our character in Christ. John 1:10 says, "If we say we have not sinned, we make Him a liar and His word is not in us." Then it goes on to say that we have propitiation or covering for our sin. But later in 1 John 3:4–7 you will note the word "practice," which means doing something over and over again. Sure we are going to sin, but that should be an aberration in our character not a thread in our character. Our perfection is not in ourselves; our perfection is in Christ. This is pointed out in Matthew 5:48, which says, "Therefore you are to be perfect, as your heavenly Father is perfect." The perfection is that we are clothed in Christ. He has covered, and continues to cover our imperfections as long as the intent of our lives is predicated upon His Lordship.

QUESTIONS AND DISCUSSION FOR THE LAW IS NOT SIN; IT IS HOLY AND SPIRITUAL

1. The Law is not _____ but through it I have a _____. (See verse 7.)

2. When sin becomes _____ we _____. (See verse 9.)

3. The commandment is _____ and _____. (See verse 12.)

4. The _____ did not cause _____ but my _____. (See verse 13.)

5. Describe the dilemma we are in with our being in the flesh and the Law being spiritual. (See verses 18–23.)

6. Who shall set us free? (See verses 24–25.) How? (See verses 4 and 6.)

Chapter 8

THE POWER OF THE GOSPEL GIVES THE CHRISTIAN POWER

ROMANS 8:1–39

Introduction

IN THE PREVIOUS chapter, Paul noted that the things he wanted to do he didn't do and the things he shouldn't do he did do. Then he says (paraphrased): "Oh, wretched man that I am. Where can I find any solace?" The seventh chapter of Romans tells us where that solace is found. Thanks to God we have victory in Christ Jesus. Now there is an energizing power within us to encourage us on this road of freedom. Let's delve into this next chapter and focus on the unleashing of the power of the Holy Spirit.

No Condemnation for Those in Christ Jesus

Romans 8:1–17

Romans 8:1 begins, "Therefore there is now no condemnation for those who are in Christ Jesus." What a difference there is between grace and the law. In the law there was no salvation, not because the law was imperfect, but because the law imputed sin. It made known what was sinful, and we made a choice to violate or keep the law of God. We have walked steadfastly in the footsteps of Adam, only things are more complex for us because there are more laws for us to violate than he possessed. The result of Adam's sin was physical death, and then Jesus' grace brought spiritual life. Thus, the Spirit of Life, rather than the spirit of sin and death, is in us when we are in Christ Jesus.

Romans 8:2: "For the law of the Spirit of life in Christ Jesus has set you free from the law of sin and of death." Free, free at last by the law of faith! What is the law of faith and grace? The law of faith is to 1) Believe in God (Hebrews 11:6). 2) Believe in the testimony concerning

God (Romans 10:17). 3) The acceptance of that testimony (Acts 17:32). 4) And obeying the instructions of the testimony (John 14:15). Are there rules to faith and grace? Sure, why would he say don't continue in sin? I thought grace was free and we were free from all rules. Grace is free in this aspect: God freely gave it. He was not obligated to do a thing for us. His love drew Him to Calvary, and Calvary gives us a response that we can freely make. We can continue to be under the obligation of the Law or under the freedom of grace (Romans 5:22–26).

Romans 8:3: "For what the Law could not do, weak as it was through the flesh, God did: sending His own Son in the likeness of sinful flesh and as an offering for sin, He condemned sin in the flesh…" This weakness Paul speaks of is not imperfection of the Law, but the imperfection or inability of man to maintain the perfection of the Law. The Law could not pay the penalty; it could but pronounce the penalty. See the difference? What God did through Jesus not only acknowledged the penalty His Law pronounced, but also made the payment for that penalty. That is the whole dynamic of the cross, the whole dynamic of His burial, and the marvelous completion of His resurrection. God satisfied the requirements of the Law for our misdeeds, and that is the law of grace.

This is further brought out in Hebrews 2:14–15: "Therefore, since the children share in flesh and blood, He Himself likewise also partook of the same, that through death He might render powerless him who had the power of death, that is, the devil, and might free those who through fear of death were subject to slavery all their lives." Here the same principle is stated in a little different manner. He recognizes that we are flesh and blood. He became flesh and blood, and through His death, He negated the power of Satan. Fear of death is only a temporal fear of departing from our normal surroundings, but we need not fear the consequences of death. Psalm 23:4 says, "Even though I walk through the valley of the shadow of death, I fear no evil, for You are with me." This doesn't say David didn't fear death, rather he did not fear the consequences of death.

Romans 8 continues (verse 4), "…so that the requirement of the Law might be fulfilled in us…" To have a relationship with God we had to keep the Law. We couldn't do this, so the relationship was fractured. But in Jesus Christ those requirements were met. When we are in Christ, we then meet the requirements of the Law—they are fulfilled in us through Christ. Verse 4 continues, "…who do not walk according to the flesh, but according to the Spirit." Notice that the word "Spirit" is capitalized. This denotes the Holy Spirit.

Romans 8:5: "For those who are according to the flesh set their minds on the things of the flesh, but those who are according to the Spirit, the things of the Spirit." When we have accepted Christ and have been joined with Him in His death, burial, and resurrection, we receive the gift of the Holy Spirit (Acts 2:38 and Acts 5:32). Inasmuch as we continue to yield our lives to the lordship of Jesus, we will be lead by the dictates of the Spirit. Verse 6 continues, "For the mind set on the flesh is death, but the mind set on the Spirit is life and peace…" Notice the fear of death, the sting of death, the power of him who has death, has been negated in the person of Jesus, and the requirement the Law demands has been satisfied by Christ. Walking in the flesh is a daily walking, not just going out boozing, carousing, cheating, lying, and so forth. It involves all that would be a violation of the Old Testament Law. No matter how good or how benevolent a person might be, or how much of a champion he or she is for human rights and for other people, his or her walk is still void of meeting the requirements of the Law. God is not going to weigh the good against the bad; this is legalism, Old Testament theology at its greatest. What God is going to weigh is what Jesus did and our acceptance of that, which then motivates us and demands of us, by the great bond of love, to live our lives in a way that is Spirit led.

Romans 8:7–8: "…because the mind set on the flesh is hostile toward God; for it does not subject itself to the law of God, for it is not even able to do so; and those who are in the flesh cannot please God." This reinforces the first and second chapters of Romans that say that all of the Gentiles and all of the Jews, regardless of how good their intentions might be, have sinned. Their inherent seed of sin goes clear back to Adam and has induced physical death in us, and that penalty must be paid.

Romans 8:9: "However, you are not in the flesh…" We are in the flesh, but that which controls the flesh is different. Our thinking, our emotions, our knowledge all are packaged up in the mind. Now our minds are going to be, not in opposition to the Law, but in harmony with grace. Grace has taken the requirement of the Law and paid for it. Though we are still in the flesh, our minds now have been clothed with Christ. We have been covered by grace. Although we still think naughty thoughts, those thoughts are not going to condemn us as they would outside of Christ, for Christ has paid the price of our weakness (Romans 1:17 and Romans 3:25). If, as these thoughts emerge, "we confess our sins, He is faithful and righteous to forgive us our sins" (see 1 John 1:8–10). Also, in 1 John 2:2 it states that we have the propitiation or the covering for those sins and that propitiation is there as long as we do not practice sin.

In the second half of verse nine we find, to the best of my knowledge, the only place in the Bible where the Spirit of God, the spirit of Christ, and the Holy Spirit are used in the same verse, and they each apply to the same Spirit. The Spirit of God, the Spirit of Christ, and the Holy Spirit are but one Spirit. Verse 9 continues, "…but in the Spirit, if indeed the Spirit of God dwells in you. But if anyone does not have the Spirit of Christ, he does not belong to Him." There is no difference between the Spirit of Christ and the Spirit of God. The thinking, knowledge, and physic of God are exactly the same as Christ's. Jesus Christ is God in the flesh. Colossians 2:9: "For in Him all the fullness of Deity dwells in bodily form." These are not different personalities but are different functions (persons) of one being. There is one God, and so the term used here is "the Spirit of God." Since only God is Holy and there is none other who is Holy but God and God is the Spirit, then His Spirit is Holy. So the Holy Spirit, the Spirit of God, and the Spirit of Christ are all brought together in perhaps the only verse in the Bible which encapsulates the concept of the Trinity so succinctly. There is only one God. The Trinity is not three separate beings; rather the Trinity is three separate functions of the same being. God functions as the Father, originator of life, protector of life, and provider of life. Christ functions as reconciler, rescuer, healer, intercessor, role model, grace giver, forgiver, justifier, and redeemer. The Spirit functions as comforter, companion, and revealer and interpreter of God's will.

Here is something beautiful to think about: when we are baptized in the name of the Father, the Son, and the Holy Spirit, we are covered by or immersed in all of the functions of God. Usually when Paul speaks of the Holy Spirit he is speaking of the function of God in a specific manner or of having this mind in you that also is in Christ Jesus (as in Philippians 2:5, where he is speaking of the Spirit of Christ). We must have that Spirit in us in order to have the mind of Christ, for the mind is the spirit of the individual. Who controls that spirit? Satan or God? If it is Satan, we are going to violate the Law and have to suffer the consequences the Law requires. If it is Christ, we then are under grace, and the requirements of the Law have already been satisfied in Christ. This to me is the "Good News" of the Gospel at its best. Here is the source of power that dwells within the Christian's heart.

Romans 8:10: "If Christ is in you, though the body is dead because of sin…" We are going to have a funeral or memorial service some day because there is death in our body due to sin. When we were born into the world, we were born pure and sinless spiritually; however, we were also born with the seed of death in us physically. At the moment of our conception, it was foreordained that we will die. Verse 10: "…yet the spirit is alive because of righteousness." This is not our righteousness, as it says in Romans 3:21, "…the righteousness of God has been manifested…" And that righteousness is in Jesus Christ. This then folds back to the proposition in Romans 1:16–17 that the power of the Gospel brings salvation. We need to think of Christ as more than just a historical figure. He said in John 16:7 (paraphrased): "It is expedient that I leave you in bodily form, because if I don't leave you, I cannot send the Comforter. In my bodily form I cannot send my Spirit, my mind, my heart into everybody."

If Christ is in you, though the body is dead because of sin, the spirit is alive because of His righteousness. Romans 8:11 says, "But if the Spirit of Him who raised Jesus from the dead dwells in you, He who raised Christ Jesus from the dead will also give life to your mortal bodies through His Spirit who dwells in you." How does He give life to our mortal bodies if our mortal bodies are dead? I would like to draw this personal illustration: Because of Christ, my body's life has been prolonged beyond that which it would have been without Christ. At the age of fifty I suffered a major coronary thrombosis that did a great deal of damage. I was given a 5% chance of survival. Without Christ, I would have croaked. I like to live on the edge of things. Without Christ, I probably would have dissipated my energies in all kinds of bad and sinful things. I may have left a wife or I may have left a half dozen kids; I wouldn't have had just three kids. I probably wouldn't have known how many kids I had or who had born them. See, I know my mindset, and I know the kind of a guy I would be without Christ. But at 80, with Christ, my life has been prolonged. He has indeed redeemed my body because it has been controlled, not by the Law, but by the Spirit of Christ. I have been able to be true to myself, true to my marriage vows, and true to God, but that is only because the Spirit of God has been implanted in my mind in place of the natural spirit of my flesh.

I am not really too keen about this physical body, especially in the last few years. Besides, this body is made up of all kinds of temporal things. It is made up of molecules, electrons, nuclei, and atoms, which, according to the third chapter of 2 Peter, all are going to go poof. Second Peter 3:7–13 says (paraphrased): "so the heavens and the earth and all that is in them shall be dissolved."

Heaven is going to be made up of that which is in corruptible. Is our body corruptible? Oh, my land, yes. Rub your tongue over your teeth, if you still have them, and you will notice all kinds of fillings, bridges, and other sorts of stuff there. This old body cannot inherit heaven, where nothing is corruptible. In 1 Corinthians 15:40–54 it says that this mortal is going to put on immortality. This terrestrial, earthy dust will put on that which is a celestial, heavenly body. Our earthly body will return to its original composition, dust. Our spirit will return to the Creator (Eccl. 12:6–7; 2 Cor. 5:17). That is good news!

Will I look the same as I do now? People recognize me by my body, but more, I hope and pray, they know me by my character. We shall be known as we are fully known (1 Cor. 13:12). Now, that is spooky, unless we know that we are in Christ and the weaknesses, flaws, and blemishes have been blotted out. People will see Christ and His character in us. That is our hope of Glory.

Romans 8:12–15 (parentheses mine): "So then, brethren, we are under obligation, not to the flesh, to live according to the flesh—for if you are living according to the flesh, you must die (our obligation); but if by the Spirit you are putting to death (a continuous action) the deeds of the body, you will live. For all who are being led by the Spirit of God (the Spirit of Christ, the mind of Christ, the Holy Spirit), these are sons of God ('sons' is used generically; ladies also are the children of God). For you have not received a spirit of slavery (that is involuntary slavery) leading to fear again, but you have received a spirit of adoption as sons by which we cry out, 'Abba! Father!'" In that great prayer that Jesus taught His disciples to pray in Matthew 6:9–13, He started out by saying (verses 9–10), "…Our Father, who art in heaven, Hollowed be Your name. Thy kingdom come, Thy will be done, on earth as it is in heaven." He was praying for the time when His will would be done on earth. And His will is done on earth when believers by faith are involved in God's grace.

Romans 8:16: "The Spirit Himself bears witness with our spirit that we are children of God…" Not only are we the children of God, which is magnificent in itself, but also, there is more! Verse 17 says, "…and if children, heirs also, heirs of God and fellow heirs with Christ, if indeed we suffer with Him in order that we may also be glorified with Him." What a verse! Everything that Jesus has inherited we are going to inherit too. I have spent time just musing over this verse, and the more I ponder it, the more I meditate over it, the more awed I become by it. I cannot even begin to comprehend the magnitude of its truth. But just because I cannot begin to understand it in the limitations of my earthly comparisons, that does not mean that I cannot believe in and enjoy and revel in that promise. Now, must we suffer with Him in order that we might be glorified with Him? I think we must. Life has its shadows, and life is going to have its heartaches and heartbreaks. There are going to be situations that are just going to rip us apart. Paul knew this; he was a man acquainted with sorrows. He probably was writing this from a jail in Caesarea, and then when he got to Rome, he wound up back in jail. He knew suffering, the hurt others can bring. He was stoned, he was left for dead, and all he did was get up and go back into the city (Acts 14:19–20).

QUESTIONS AND DISCUSSION FOR NO CONDEMNATION FOR THOSE IN CHRIST JESUS

1. There is no _____ those in _____. (See verse 1.)

2. The law of the _____ of _____ free from the _____ and _____. (See verse 2.)

3. Where is the weakness of the law? How was it rectified? (See verse 3.)

4. What is the determining factor that separates us from walking in the flesh and being in the spirit? (See verses 9–11. Also note Acts 2:38; 5:32; Rom. 6:3–11.)

5. How is the resurrection of Christ of importance to us? (See verse 11.)

6. Where is the source of power to put to death the works of the flesh? (See verse 13.)

7. The _____ of God are those led by the _____. (See verse 14.)

8. Who is the witness to us that we are God's children? (See verse 16.)

9. As a child of God we become an heir of _____ and a joint heir of _____ (verse 17).

The Help of the Spirit in Times of Suffering

Romans 8:18–39

Romans 8:18: "For I consider that the sufferings of this present time are not worthy to be compared with the glory that is to be revealed to us." Paul said this after he was mocked, rebuked, and betrayed. We each have trials and sufferings. They are very personal, very real, and very disturbing. I know; I have been there. I have tough times, and I know the anxiety involved. None of us have shared in all of the suffering that Jesus shared in. Look at your hands for a minute. Do you see any place where a nail went through them? As servants, should we expect better treatment than the Master? "But if we suffer with Him, we shall be glorified with Him." These verses (Romans 8:18–39) brings such confidence in times of adversity because it states that our problems, whether they are intellectual, emotional, or physical, are just not comparable to the glory that shall be revealed to us. Generally speaking, we think of that glory in the hereafter. I would like us to consider that as we grow in Christ, He becomes more the anchor of our hearts and the object of our faith. The more He is revealed to us, the more we place into a proper perspective the adversities of a moment. That glorification is so much greater than the momentary suffering that it isn't even worthy of the comparison. This is the hope that comes with salvation.

Here are some companion scriptures to Romans 8:17 and 18. They are found in 2 Corinthians 4:16–17: "Therefore we do not lose heart, but though our outer man is decaying, yet our inner man is being renewed day by day. For momentary, light affliction is producing for us an eternal weight of glory far beyond all comparison." Our afflictions don't seem momentary or light. But if we consider the weight of eternal glory and imagine placing this weight and the weight of each of our burdens on a teeter-totter, our burdens would be flung so high in the air that they would still be spinning. The eternal weight of glory is far beyond all comparison.

Second Corinthians 4:18 and 5:1–5 go on to say, "…while we look not at the things which are seen, but at the things which are not seen; for the things which are seen are temporal, but the things which are not seen are eternal" (2 Cor. 4:18). "For we know that if the earthly tent which is our house is torn down, we have a building from God, a house not made with hands (not of human origin), eternal in the heavens. For indeed in this house we groan, longing to be clothed with our dwelling from heaven; inasmuch as we, having put it on, shall not be found naked. For indeed while we are in this tent, we groan, being burdened, because we do not want to be unclothed, but to be clothed, so that what is mortal will be swallowed up by life. Now He who prepared us for this very purpose is God, who gave to us the Spirit as a pledge" (2 Cor. 5:1–5, parentheses mine). The life we have in Christ is a pledge by God, promising us that which is eternal in the heavens. But we don't need to wait until we get to heaven to see the glories being revealed to us. As we grow in Christ those glories are beginning to percolate, matriculate through our systems. These glories ultimately shall find their fullness in heaven, but there is such a great, great joy in just being a Christian and in living the Christian life. It is phenomenal. Assume, hypothetically, that there is no heaven. Just to be a Christian and to live that life with the Spirit of God within us is sufficient. Imagine His buoying us when the old ship begins to lean one way or another and we lose our balance; just that would make being a Christian worthwhile. Even if heaven was taken away, just being a Christian for today and seeing how our lives grow and matriculate in His grace and in His glory is sufficient for us to reach out and long to walk with Christ. We know and we believe with such a great conviction in God's promises. And heaven is thrown in to boot!

Romans 8:19: "For the anxious longing of the creation waits eagerly for the revealing of the sons of God." This does not apply to physical creation apart from man, rather it is talking about the creation that spiritually was ruined by sin, but now has been regained. Consider the illustration that when we were babes we were born spiritually pure and free. That is the way we were born. The spiritual death that came in to us had nothing to do with Adam except that we have inherited the tendency to sin; rather our spiritual death is due to our own falling. Verses 20–21: "For the creation was subjected to futility, not willingly, but because of Him who subjected it, in hope that the creation itself also will be set free from its slavery to corruption into the freedom of the glory of the children of God." The penalty on Adam and Eve's sin was first rendered to Satan, second to Eve, third to Adam, and fourth to creation (Genesis 3).

The penalty to creation would be weeds in the world; creation did not know weeds before the pollution of sin entered (Gen. 3:17–19). The principle of pollution due to the greed of man is still in effect today. The beauty of our earth is spoiled by the greed of people, as the air, water, and ground itself are being molested by the sins of man.

Romans 8:22: "For we know that the whole creation groans and suffers the pains of childbirth together until now." Not only has the populace of the world, but also the world itself has a negative reaction to the sins of man. Our environment has become a popular theme of our day. That is the general and most accepted appreciation of these verses. Let's consider a different standpoint, looking from the context of the individual and our struggle with sin. Remember the seventh chapter of Romans, which says "I want to do right and I don't and the things I don't want to do I do." Gee, where is my victory? The victory is in Christ. Remember the sixth chapter of Romans, where we lost our involuntary servitude to Satan for a voluntary enslavement to the lordship of God's grace? That has been the theme of the sixth and seventh chapters, and we can place these verses within that theme. The creation of man is not his physical being. God formed man from the dust. Formation and creation are two different things. To form is to take that which already exists and to remold, reshape, rearrange, reprogram; that is, a formation of our physical origins. Man was *formed* from the dust of the earth. Man became God's creation when He breathed life into that which He had formed (Gen. 2:7). Thus He created man in

His own image (Gen. 1:26–27). God does not have physical limitations or time restraints. The initial creation in our mind and in our heart is limited only by the formation that surrounds it. That formation gets a little older every orbit about the sun. Consequently, we are inhibited from doing the things that we want, but our minds can spring out beyond human adversities and physical handicaps. Some of the most inspiring people that I have ever met, talked with, and prayed with have been people who have had great physical adversities.

Years back, at an intersection in a small west coast town in Oregon, there was a country store where Mr. Johnson was the proprietor. We had the opportunity of going in there because Mr. Johnson was interested in coming to the Lord. While sharing Christ with him, I felt like I wasn't giving the blessing. Rather, I felt like I was receiving the blessing. When I went in there, I found a double amputee in a wheelchair with just a stub of a leg on each side. I also found a man whose creative mind, spirit, and heart were so alive, so optimistic, and so positive. He wanted to reach out to know the source that gave him a great outlook in life.

In one congregation, we had a blind lady who later moved to an adjacent state. I appreciated her. She always sat right next to the isle in the second pew and was a source of inspiration as I tried to preach. I could see her reading her Braille Bible right along with me, even though she couldn't see a thing. Whenever I would pray with her or talk with her, I always came away feeling as though I shortchanged her. I was ministered to far more than I ministered.

We can apply the mastering of human suffering to creation, not so much to the birds, the bees, the trees, and so forth, although that may have merit, but to people. When we come to Christ, we become new creatures in Christ. The creative part of us, which was created in the image of God, takes on a new entity, like it was in the beginning—not because of my meritorious good works, but because of Jesus' sacrificial good works. I would like to think of this creation in the sense of a personal change within the life of an individual. Also, I think of this creation as it refers to the creation that is in Christ, the futility of that creation out of Christ, and the benefit of that creation in Jesus Christ.

Let's get back to Romans. Romans 8:23 says, "And not only this, but also we ourselves, having the first fruits of the Spirit, even we ourselves groan within ourselves, waiting eagerly for our adoption as sons, the redemption of our body." We in Christ are new creatures in Him (2 Cor. 5:17). This old creation, which has been spoiled, longs for redemption, longs for the day when we see Christ face to face.

Our sinfulness has a trickle-down effect. Not only is sin found within man, but also it trickles down into all of the aspects of creation—for there is rot, there is death, there is erosion, and there is deterioration in almost every aspect of creation. This is a result, in part, of the constant sin of man and the abuse by man of our natural resources, motivated primarily by greed or politics or both. Yet we long to see a beginning of a new creation so that it can trickle down and have an effect upon all matter and material.

This position of being a Christian is weighty. We need to think beyond ourselves. We become so introverted in our Christian experience that we fail to realize the impact that a Christian has in this world. I talked to a fellow named Tom over in the Inland Empire, and he said, "You know, you can look at a nation and tell how free Christianity has been in that country by the society that has been formed." If you have a globe, give it a spin, then hold your finger near the surface, and if that globe stops over land, look at the country and gage that country by how freely Christianity has been propagated there. It really won't be hard for you to determine by the society and the philosophy that guards and keeps that nation whether or not Christ has had free reign in its borders. It will spill out.

There is a lot in this little verse (Romans 8:23) regarding creation groaning. You and I have a greater impact than we would ever dream, even if it is in just one vote. Our influence, because we hold the standards of morality, the standards that are inherent within the wool and fiber of our character due to the presence of Christ, can be tremendous. God expects us to rescue the world, not only spiritually, but also environmentally.

Romans 8:24–25: "For in hope we have been saved, but hope that is seen is not hope; for who hopes for what he already sees? But if we hope for what we do not see, with perseverance we wait eagerly for it." If I hoped for $13 million and got it, I wouldn't have to hope for $13 million any more. But I would hope for more, say $20 million. But if I hoped for thirteen kids and had them, I sure wouldn't hope for any more. Not only does the Spirit work in us, but also He is part of us. What more is there to hope for? He is the water of life that will cause us to thirst no more (John 4).

Romans 8:26: "And in the same way the Spirit also helps our weakness…" This covers all areas and facets of the weaknesses of every personality—mine are different from yours, and yours are different from mine. The Spirit helps us in our weaknesses, if we allow Him to work in our lives. As we recognize our weaknesses and seek His help and guidance in those weaknesses, He has promised to assist us. So which weakness are we going to talk about first? Where do we start? The answer could kind of surprise you.

Let's look at the rest of verse: "…for we do not know how to pray as we should, but the Spirit Himself intercedes for us with groanings too deep for words…" So the Spirit helps us in our prayers! Should we pray in ignorance? You bet! In most of our prayers, as far as the scope and magnitude of what we are asking and the details regarding those circumstances, we are ignorant.

There are other things to consider when we pray. For instance, if the subject is really personal to us, then it behooves us to determine how honest we are with ourselves. Also, remember that when we pray for someone who is ill or pray for somebody who is having an emotional problem, we just know the general parameters; we don't know the miniscule details. We don't know the depth of agony, the depth of hurt, the depth of sorrow, the depth of frustration. Oh, the person can tell us, but we still can't empathize to the degree that we can really get right in and see where that person is going, because he or she has so many other factors in his or her life that are going to govern that.

In addition, we can make this determination: that we pray in accordance with our vision, and our vision is much better in retrospect than for projecting the future. We don't know what lies ahead for the balance of this day, let alone for our tomorrows. Many times we borrow the anxieties of tomorrow and carry them today. Those anxieties might be 90% unrealized, because when we speculate on things, unfortunately, sometimes we dream and speculate on the worst types of scenarios that can possibly come about. But God knows our hearts even better than we do. When God searches our hearts, He sees and knows those things we find impossible to place into words, either through ignorance or through extreme elation or because of extreme remorse. With a communication that is beyond our vocabulary, the Spirit makes the utterance and intercedes for us, because He knows the heart that we have. We may be misunderstood, we may misunderstand, but that is a part of human experience. God knows the heart!

When looking at this passage, there are many who interpret the "groanings" as speaking in tongues. Nowhere in this context is that brought up, and to insert that in one phrase is ludicrous. In my opinion, doing so is a grave injustice and is borrowing from a scripture out of context to prove a proposition that may have no merit. Rather, these "groanings" are the Holy Spirit helping us to pray as we should and helping with the gut feelings we have that we can't express.

This intercession is a tremendous service that the Holy Spirit provides. God knows our hearts. When we pray, even though it may largely be in ignorance or in very limited vision, God is going to be there, and He is going to work for us. That is why so many "coincidences" happen when we pray; and it is amazing how few coincidences happen when we fall back from praying. Now that is a coincidence, isn't it?

Romans 8:27: "…and He who searches the hearts knows what the mind of the Spirit is, because He intercedes for the saints according to the will of God." What a blessed reassurance to us that God's will can be accomplished in our lives. We don't have to struggle alone. His will shall be done. Because of this, we can know that all things work together according to His will, all of God's works. When we pray and bare our hearts before Him, just really dump the load and let God's will start to fill us, then good things happen. One caution: We must be very, very careful in our prayers, and I am talking to old Ted here too, that we don't try to manipulate the answer to prayer. That is not good—that is not good at all.

Romans 8:28: "And we know that God causes all things to work together for good to those who love God, to those who are called according to His purpose." That is another one of those good verses isn't it? What constitutes the calling of God for His purpose? Recall Romans 1:16–17, which says, "For I am not ashamed of the Gospel, for it is the power of God for salvation to everyone who believes, to the Jew first and also to the Greek. For in it the righteousness of God is revealed from faith to faith; as it is written, '*but the righteous man shall live by faith.*'" The calling by God is seen in the whole ministry, purpose, teaching, and triumph of Jesus Christ. He calls us to Him through Him. That is God's calling, and the purpose of that calling is that you and I can enjoy an intimate, close, real spiritual relationship with God. This is the bottom line. All things work together for good. Now, in the limitations of our human flesh, we can interfere with the good being accomplished by God. But if we come in prayer, in some way, God is going to work through our limitations in a manner we did not envision or we did not plan or that wasn't according to our script but was according to God's will. We can see it in little things. God's hand is working because the Spirit intercedes. He knows our hearts, and He intercedes on our behalf. This is the real beauty of this verse.

Romans 8:29: "For those whom He foreknew, He also predestined to become conformed to the image of His Son, so that He would be the firstborn among many brethren..." "Predestination" and "foreordination" (or "foreknowledge") are two fancy, big theological words. Let's see if we can't simplify this. I am going to draw an illustration, a crummy illustration, but maybe it will parallel this so we can see it.

Let's say it is about ten at night and the news is on until about 10:15. I don't care about all that negative news, so I will just wait until 10:15 to turn on the TV, because that is when the weather man is going to make a report. The weather is what I want to hear because that really affects me. So this weatherman has his visual aids. They've got satellites up there, and they can tell the pressure and where the density and the highness and the lowness are. "Here we can see a band of highs out here," he says. "Now, by 2:00 tomorrow afternoon it is going to start raining." That is foreknowledge, at least to the best of his ability that is foreknowledge. But did that weather man cause all of that stuff on the chart? No. That is predestination. It was predetermined that it is going to rain. It was because of certain factors that he could foretell it is going to rain.

Likewise, when God calls a person through the Gospel and that person responds to that call, He knows by that response that that person is His child. He foreknows that we will break through the high pressure of pride and the stubbornness of self to the point that we come to repent and then share with Him in that new life in His death, burial, and resurrection—He knows that we will be His. He foreknows that those who do that will be His because He predetermined, before the foundation of the world was laid, a means by which we could have this salvation. So it is the scheme, the plan of salvation that leads us into a relationship that was predestined. When we become Christians, we enter into a predestined state or condition. It is predestined that we shall be heirs and joint heirs with Christ Jesus, that heaven is our home. It is predestined as long as we are in relationship with Him through Jesus. We are predestined, and we will go to heaven because we are already in the conveyance that was predestined to take us there.

Here is another illustration: I've got to get up to the fourth floor of the Loma Linda Hospital, because that is where the Cardiac floor is. So I stand in front of an elevator. I get into an elevator. I answer the call. The call of that elevator is that it stops and it opens the door and the arrow points up. As soon as I get in, the elevator foreknows that I am going to the fourth floor because I hit the button that says "4" on it. So that elevator has been predestined by design and engineering to take me there. This to me is a correlation of foreordination and predestination, or foreknowledge and predestination.

I am really uncomfortable with the concept that we are here and our every step is planned and predestined by God, implying that we have no choice. I think: When are we chosen and when are we predestined? When do we become the chosen people of God? When we become the chosen people of God, we are predestined for an eternity with God. This thought is developed in Romans 11. But let's just say here that the means of our obtaining a relationship with God was predestined before the foundation of the world was laid. When we by faith enter into a relationship with God, we enter into that predestined means of salvation that God has provided. Our being chosen as His people is based upon the faith we exercise when we yield to the lordship of Jesus. I think that to come to any other conclusion would do irreparable damage to the concept that God created us in His image.

The image of God is a self-determining entity, and for us to be created in the image of anything other than a self-determined entity is a felonious position. God foresees a whole lot more than we can imagine. He knows our lives from the moment we are conceived until the time that we die, but that does not mean that He is going to personally intervene in the choice that we make regarding our relationship with Him. His intervention is often by placing circumstances in our pathway that demand resolution. Those demands are met by our free choice, and we bear the consequences of our choices. If our choices are contrary to divine principle, it is unfair of us to place those consequences at the feet of God. This is why we pray, "Lord lead us not into temptation" (Matthew 6:13), because He knows how much we can endure. This is why it says that, "He will not tempt us beyond that which we are capable of enduring, but will make a way of escape" (1 Cor. 10:13). He is not going to push us out the exit when the house is on fire, but He will provide an exit and hope that you will make the choice to use it. We dare not limit the omniscience and omnipotence of God. I am really uncomfortable when we bring God down into the limitations of time and matter.

Romans 8:30–31: "...and these whom He predestined, He also called; and these whom He called, He also justified; and these whom He justified, He also glorified. What then shall we say to these things?" What is going to be our response to the calling of God to enter into a predetermined divine plan? Let's look at the rest of Romans 8:31, where Paul answers this question: "If God is for us, who is against us? He who did not spare His own Son, but delivered Him over for us all, how will He not also with Him freely give us all things?" If

God paid the payment Himself upon the cross, who is it that can stand against God or His people? In 1John 4:4 it says, "…greater is He who is in you than he who is in the world." Pull your shoulders back Christian. Lift your head up high. Because of Jesus, we can and have defeated Satan.

Romans 8:33: "Who will bring a charge against God's elect?" God's elect are those who have answered the call and in so doing are the chosen of God. How will anybody bring a charge against us, because when we answered the call and were chosen by God we were justified by God. That justification is greater than Satan's condemnation. Verses 33 and 34 continue, "God is the one who justifies; who is the one who condemns? Christ Jesus is He who died, yes, rather who was raised, who is at the right hand of God, who also intercedes for us." Who can condemn in the light of that fact? What can condemn? What rights do I, or any religious leaders or any religious institutions, have to determine who will and who will not go to heaven?

Verse 35: "Who will separate us from the love of Christ?" Not only does Paul get to the "whom," but also he gets to the "what" before we get through with this. First of all, he talks about physical things as we continue in verse 35: "Will tribulation, or distress, or persecution, or famine, or nakedness, or peril, or sword?" All of these have to do with the abuse of the body, threats against your life, against your health. Verses 36–37: "Just as it is written, *'for your sake we are being put to death all day long; we were considered as sheep to be slaughtered.'* But in all these things we overwhelmingly conquer through Him who loved us." There is no physical trial that in and of itself can separate you from the will of God, unless you let it. Now Paul is going to get into a few intangibles. Verses 38–39 say, "For I am convinced that neither death, nor life, nor angels, nor principalities, nor things present, nor things to come, nor powers, nor height, nor depth, nor any other created thing, shall be able to separate us from the love of God, which is in Christ Jesus our Lord." There are no sets of spiritual entities that have the power to separate us from the love of God. There are no sets of physical circumstances that in and of themselves are able to separate us from the love of God that is in Christ Jesus. If we keep the faith, we are unconquerable. Bless the Lord, oh my soul! And it is all there because of the presence of the Lord Jesus Christ. What a rich, powerful, wonderful, uplifting, joy-filled chapter that should instill within each one of us huge degrees of confidence as we walk with God!

QUESTIONS AND DISCUSSION FOR THE HELP OF THE SPIRIT IN TIMES OF SUFFERING

1. One qualification is to _____ with Him. The reward is _____. (See verse 18.)

THE POWER OF THE GOSPEL GIVES THE CHRISTIAN POWER

2. The answer of creation's plight and hope. Depend upon _____.
    (See verse 19–22.)

3. The source of hope is our being the _____. (See verses 23–25.)

4. The _____ helps us in the weakness of our _____.
    (See verse 26.)

5. The weakness of our prayers is _____. (See verses 26–28.)

6. What is the difference between foreknowledge and predestination? (See verse 29.)

7. To what have we been predestined? What is the progression? (See verse 30.)
    1 _____ 2 _____ 3 _____

8. How has God demonstrated He is for us? (See verses 31–32.)

9. Why is it foolish to bring a charge against Gods elect? (See verse 33.)

10. Why is condemnation not possible? (See verse 34.)

11. Name physical or spiritual things that cannot separate us from God. (See verses 35–39.)

WE OVERWHELMINGLY CONQUER THROUGH HIM.

Chapter 9

THE JEWS, THE ONLY CHILDREN OF GOD? NO!

ROMANS 9:1–33

Introduction

RECALL PAUL DESCRIBING himself as a bond-servant (Rom. 1:1). One might think that is just rhetoric. But in this chapter we are going to see how much conviction he had about being a bond-servant. We are going to take a look into the very depth of Paul's character and heart. Usually we think of him as a hard-driving, hardnosed—John Mark you go home; you copped out on us once, and I am not going to take you again— very aggressive sort of a guy. But the man had a heart just as big as this whole world, and he was extremely sensitive. He had a compassion and love for people we would do well to emulate. This is immediately evident as we get into this chapter.

Paul's Great Compassion for Israel

Romans 9:1–13

In Romans 8 we saw that we are joint heirs with Christ. We found out that the Holy Spirit intercedes for us and helps us in our weakness, particularly in the area of prayer. Also, we discovered that we can receive great victory over material and spiritual things. One of Paul's concluding statements was, "But in all these things we overwhelmingly conquer through Him who loved us" (Romans 8:37). In light of what is in the eighth chapter and of everything that has been brought out based on our foundational premise of this book, we see now that the Gospel is the power of God unto salvation and includes all those who follow our acceptance of Christ Jesus.

Romans 9:1 begins, "I am telling the truth in Christ…" This truth that he is telling is so way out, so non-humanistic, so departed from the self-centeredness and self-interest of individuals that he adds further emphasis by saying (verse 1), "…I am not lying, my conscience testifies with me in the Holy Spirit…" Paul is about to declare something that is really unusual and different. Verse 2: "…that I have great sorrow and unceasing grief in my heart." While he already led us in the eighth chapter to the very mountaintop of ecstasy, now Paul finds himself in a position where he has great sorrow and unceasing grief.

Romans 9:3: "For I could wish that I myself were accursed, separated from Christ for the sake of my brethren, my kinsmen according to the flesh…" Paul talked about God's Grace and how nothing can separate us, about being an heir, and yet he has such love and compassion for his fellow Jews. These are the same Jews who not only persecuted him and put him in jail, but also ran him out of town and stoned him. Yet, he says he has such a love for them that if throwing off his salvation, which he rejoiced in so greatly, would bring them to Christ, he would do it. No wonder he said, "I am a bond-servant." But he didn't just say it. Here in the very depth of it he puts this servitude into practice. This is really no more than what his Master did for all of us, is it? We read in 2 Corinthians 8:9, "…that though He was rich, yet for your sake He became poor, that you through His poverty might become rich." Philippians 2:5–6 says that Jesus had this mind in Him that being in the existence of God wasn't something He had to hold on to. Position and privilege were not something He needed to follow or conform to. He was willing to let go to become as we are, even to the point of death. Paul said that he would be willing to serve others and be as a bond-servant because he did not consider himself greater than the Master.

This is the attitude we really need to have restored in our Christian faith and in the church, especially in the leadership of the church. We need a heart of compassion, where we don't expect to be ministered to but are willing to give of ourselves, without a thought of award or merit, so that others might be saved. Sometimes we get so caught up in our own self-importance that we lose sight of the lost.

So Romans 9 starts out pretty deep, getting down to what being a servant of God is about in its very lowest and yet very highest form. Romans 9:4–5 continues Paul's thoughts, "… who are Israelites, to whom belongs the adoption as sons, and the glory and the covenants and the giving of the Law and the temple service and the promises, whose are the fathers, and from whom is the Christ according to the flesh, who is over all, God blessed forever, Amen." The Israelites had tremendous opportunities. They possessed the adoption as sons. They had the glory of being the children of God's promise. They had the custodianship of the Law, and the benefits of keeping that Law would be heaped upon them. They were able to have all the joys and pleasures of temple service and the worship of God and the maintaining of those God-given rites and ordinances intended to further their relationship with God. They were the recipients of the promises God made. They had a great heritage, which was handed down from generation to generation. The Messiah's earthly lineage came through Israel—this Messiah who would come in the flesh to be over all, God blessed forever! What a privilege to be called a Jew! It was a great and lofty position. But they botched it all up. They got caught up in their self-importance and forgot the purpose for which God had given all those things to them.

Verse 6: "But it is not as though the word of God has failed." Nor was God a failure in granting all this to them, as it wasn't God who failed. Verse 6 continues (here Paul makes a shift), "For they are not all Israel who are descended from Israel…" That is a weighty statement. The Israelites are not the only ones who should be considered as recipients of the entire heritage expressed in the fourth and fifth verses. And they were not all children just because they are Abraham's descendents, as the children of promise are regarded as descendents. The children of the flesh were counted as descendents as long as they had faith. And when faith is exercised by those who are not fleshly descendents, they become Israelites by faith. For we read in Galatians 3:29, "And if you belong to Christ, then you are Abraham's offspring, heirs according to promise."

One fundamental problem we have today is that we have failed to make this transition between the physical situations of the Old Testament and how they are applied in principle to the spiritual relationships of the New Testament. A failure to make this transition causes us to apply spiritual dynamics back to the temporal or physical consequence of the Old Testament. One of the things that really affected my theology and my thinking was coming to the understanding that almost every major event and every major personality in the Old Testament was a prototype of principle or a forerunner of Jesus Christ. When we are in Christ, then, the spiritual application needs to be made rather than the physical.

There are a lot of people who find the times in the Old Testament when God commanded the Israelites to go capture a city and kill every child, every woman, every animal—the whole business—disturbing regarding the justice of God. From a spiritual standpoint, with sin and Satan in our lives and hearts, this is exactly what God wants us to do—destroy it all. He uses the physical dynamic to illustrate the spiritual dynamic we are to exercise when we become Christians. That is a part of accepting Jesus as the Lord of our lives. When we understand some of the dynamics of the Old Testament, which would be considered, even by non-Christians, to be extremely barbaric, we find a proper equivalent as we apply it to the spiritual things of today.

The Jews missed the first advent of Christ because they were looking for a physical king. Jesus' reestablishing a kingdom here, rebuilding Jerusalem, and having peace on earth for 1,000 years are all earth-orientated. From a second coming standpoint, we haven't shifted gears yet. Once we grasp that concept and start reading and looking at the Scriptures, seeking connections, it is really, really fantastic, as it all fits and ties together without any inconsistencies.

Romans 9:7–9: "…nor are they all children because they are Abraham's descendants, but: '*Through isaac your descendants will be named.*' That is, it is not the children of the flesh who are children of God, but the children of the promise are regarded as descendants. For this is a word of promise: '*At this time I will come, and sarah shall have a son.*'" That is the promise.

Romans 9:10–11: "And not only this, but there was Rebekah also, when she had conceived twins by one man, our father Isaac; for though the twins were not yet born and had not done anything good or bad, in order that God's purpose according to His choice might stand, not because of works, but because of Him who calls…" Now we see the matter of predestination, starting to rear its head. Verse 12: "…it was said to her, '*the older will serve the younger.*'" This is a pattern that we have seen over and over again.

Let's stop and think for a moment about the relationship between the first and second and the greatest and least. Jesus said, "Whoever wishes to be first among you shall be your slave" (Matthew 19:27), and note (Mark 10:43–44). Again, Isaac was the second son of Abraham, Ishmael was the first. The last became first. Esau was the first of the twins to be born, Jacob was second. He who was last became first. Saul, the Benjaminite, was the first king. Jonathan, his son, made a covenant to serve David. David was the last son, but he became the greatest, the king. The Gospel was first preached to the Jews and then to the Gentiles, so similarly the last became the greater children of God, because of faith. These incidences in the Scriptures, as they are predestined by God, serve the purpose of bringing the picture of redemption into full view.

Romans 9:12–13: "…it was said to her, '*the older will serve the younger.*' Just as it is written, '*jacob I loved, but esau I hated.*'" This was determined even before they were born, as it is indicated in verse 11. It wasn't based upon merit, not because of works, "but because of Him who calls." Now this isn't exactly the same as it is in Ishmael and Isaac's case, because the one was the son of promise and the other the son of promiscuousness, but the overall depiction and principle are the same.

QUESTIONS AND DISCUSSION FOR PAUL'S GREAT COMPASSION FOR ISRAEL

1. Following is a statement of _____ witnessed by the _____ (verse 1).

2. Great _____ and _____ in his _____ (verse 2).

3. Longing so great for his _____ that he willing be _____ from _____ (verse 3).

4. Name 8 things that belong to the Israelites (verses 4–5).

5. The children of God are the children of _____ not of the _____. (See verse 8.)

6. How is God justified in extending the promise through Jacob? (See verses 10–13.)

Objections Israel Raised and Paul's Response to Them

Romans 9:14–33

Romans 9:14–15: "What shall we say then? There is no injustice with God, is there? May it never be! For He says to Moses, '*I will have mercy on whom I have mercy, and I will have compassion on whom I have compassion.*'" God's acts are not acts of injustice. God has a right to show mercy to whom He chooses. This is the privilege of God. God also has a right to withhold mercy from whom He will or chooses. As we look about us and see in the world tremendous injustice we must not lay that at the feet of God. Injustice is the result of sin-filled man.

Romans 9:16: "So then it does not depend on the man who wills or the man who runs, but on God who has mercy." This is really important. If God knew us in the womb, before we were born, surely a God with that power could have a plan that our life is to follow—not one He micromanages, but a plan with the freedom of choice. Let me make a suggestion. There are incidences where predestination has been enacted on people by God. Predestination means to be predetermined by God that they should act accordingly and that they have no say in that area. There are some who feel, with a great base of merit, that Pharaoh of Egypt walked a predestined path. After every event God hardened his heart (Exodus 7–11). Romans 9:17–18 says, "For the Scripture says to Pharaoh, '*for this very purpose I raised you up, to demonstrate my power in you, and that my name might be proclaimed throughout the whole earth.*' So then He has mercy on whom He desires, and He hardens whom He desires."

Based on the above, we can reach this conclusion: In a very narrow application, predestination is tied to providing for the predetermined plan of our redemption or reconciliation. God has, on certain occasions, predestined people to fulfill their lives in order that His plan might be completed. However, this is not a universal practice, but it is used only when tied to that predetermined plan of reconciliation. If God acted that way in all cases, then we would have a problem with forgiveness. In addition to that, God would then become a God who predestines murder, rape, incest, and all kinds of satanic activities. That is not the kind of God who serves the world in love and whom we serve. Further, it is not consistent with all the other principles of our faith and self-determination, thus predestination cannot be applied outside of that narrow parameter. For example, I am uncomfortable with the idea that it was predestined for me to be a preacher regardless of what I did. This removes free choice. I believe that I could have made a different choice, and the plan was that whatever choice I made I would reap the fruits of that choice, whether succulent and delicious or bitter and rotten.

There is a difference between foreknowledge and foreordination. Foreordination would be God not giving us any leeway for free choice. However, He may foreknow what we will do and choose not to interfere with our choices, but still foreordain the consequences of those choices. God's plan is that none would perish, but because of individual choice, some do. Still, God's plan remains the same; that is, He is not willing that any should perish (2 Peter 3:8–9). We make choices that separate us from God, but the plan doesn't change. God's plan through Christ remains exactly as it has always been. Our acceptance of and obedience to that plan is a free choice. But too often we make all kinds of choices that are in opposition to God's plan. In the creation of the salvation plan there are occasions where God did predestine people to act in the way they did (e.g. Pharaoh and Esau and Judas). Situations like these are not the general practice or rule but are complying with the orchestration of God's preordained or predestined plan. Again, verse 18 says, "So then He has mercy on whom He desires, and He hardens whom He desires." As we look at this and the narrow framework we have discussed regarding predestination, remember that God has a right to show mercy and God has a right to withhold mercy as He wills.

Romans 9:19–23: "You will say to me then, 'Why does He still find fault? For who resists His will?' On the contrary, who are you, O man, who answers back to God? The thing molded will not say to the molder, 'Why did you make me like this,' will it? Or does not the potter have a right over the clay, to make from the same lump one vessel for honorable use and another for common use? What if God, although willing to demonstrate His wrath and to make His power known, endured with much patience vessels of wrath prepared for destruction? And He did so to make known the riches of His glory upon vessels of mercy, which He prepared beforehand for glory…" The riches of His glory that He has made known are the matters of justification and reconciliation. I think these verses sum it all up and shed a little light on where we fit into God's will for our lives.

Romans 9:24: "…even us, whom He also called, not from among Jews only, but also from among Gentiles." Paul then quotes a prophecy from Hosea in verses 25–26: "As He says also in Hosea, '*I will call those who were not my people, "my people," and her who was not beloved, "beloved." And it shall be that in the place where it was said to them, "you are not my people," there they shall be called sons of the living god.*'" So, that which was second, now through spiritual means, exchanges place with that which was first.

Next Paul quotes some prophecies from Isaiah. Romans 9:27: "And Isaiah cries out concerning Israel, '*though the number of the sons of israel be like the sand of the sea, it is the remnant that will be saved…*'" (Isa. 10:22). Physically, they are like the sands of the sea, but from a salvation standpoint, from Christ forward, it becomes only a remnant of those Jewish folks who will be saved. Why is this? It is because of their lack of faith. Notice how this plays out. Romans 9:28–30 (parentheses mine) continues, "'...*for the lord will execute his word on the earth, thoroughly and quickly.*' And just as Isaiah foretold, '*unless the lord of sabaoth* (or the Lord of the finish or the last) *had left to us a posterity* (they had a great heritage), *we would have become like sodom, and would have resembled gomorrah.*' What shall we say then? That Gentiles, who did not pursue righteousness, attained righteousness, even the righteousness which is by faith..." It was the Jewish people who were pursuing righteousness by the Law, and that is illustrated in verse 31: "...but Israel, pursuing a law of righteousness, did not arrive at that law." This was through no weakness of the Law; actually, it was the perfection of the Law that was their stumbling block, because of the weakness of the flesh. Verse 32 continues, "Why? Because they did not pursue it by faith, but as though it were by works. They stumbled over the stumbling stone..." See how this folds back to Romans 9:16? It "does not depend on the man who wills or the man who runs (which would fit the Jew, wouldn't it?), but on God who has mercy."

Paul then quotes Isaiah again in verse 33: "...just as it is written, '*behold, I lay in zion a stone of stumbling...*'" This quote is found in Isaiah 28:16, which says, "Therefore thus says the Lord GOD, 'Behold, I am laying in Zion a stone, a tested stone, A costly cornerstone for the foundation, firmly placed. He who believes in it will not be disturbed.'" A tested or trying stone in some translations is a costly cornerstone. That stone they stumbled over. Notice the attribute of the stone; it is the foundational stone, the chief cornerstone. It is the stone that was tried and tested. Now, I ask the question again: What is this stone being built upon? Christ! He became the stumbling stone, but it wasn't laid for them to stumble over, it was laid for them to build upon, for a cornerstone is the key stone in a building. Every other stone in the building is placed in reference to the cornerstone or built in relation to the cornerstone. Christ is the cornerstone of the kingdom, and God sent Jesus to lay a foundation to be built upon, but instead, they stumbled on that very stone. They tried to build on the letter of the Law rather than upon God, who fulfills the Law and assumed the penalty the Law demanded.

I was leading a group of folks in Jerusalem, and I got a little excited when we got up to the temple mount. I wanted to draw their attention to the mosque with the golden dome glistening in the afternoon sun. I wanted to point up there, and I started backing up. There was a big stone behind me that I did not see. I backed into that stone, and I went every way but upright. I had appendages going in every direction. When I opened my eyes, there was blue sky above. This scripture came to mind: "...there was a stumbling stone..." This was exactly what the Jewish people did. In the very heart of that which they could build upon, they instead became an offense. Verse 33 says, "...*and a rock of offense, and he who believes in him will not be disappointed.*" That "rock" was Jesus, who gave His life for His kinsmen.

As this chapter of Romans shows, the Jews had the heritage and all of the opportunities, and yet they fell flat on their face because they did not come by faith. So enters a people not called beloved who become beloved, a people not called His own, but now they are God's children. Here they come, a people who did not pursue it but who built upon that stone, and it became to them salvation. This great chapter plows deep and really shows that our reconciliation to God is not due to our ancestry but due to our faith. And more importantly, we have a free choice to make it so.

QUESTIONS AND DISCUSSION FOR OBJECTIONS ISRAEL RAISED AND PAUL'S RESPONSE TO THEM

1. Do we have a right to question God's will? _____ If not, why not? _____ _____ (verses 4–18).

2. Our relationship with God is dependent on _____ (verse16).

3. Was Pharaoh predestined to his fate? If so, why? (See verses 17–18.)

4. What illustration is used to disallow us from questioning Gods judgment? (See verses19–24.)

5. Fulfillment of a prophecy found in _____ (verses 25–26).

6. Three gems of wisdom from _____ are _____ _____ (verses 27–29).

7. How do verses 30–32 refer back to the principle seen in verse16?

8. What do you think the stumbling stone is referring to as it is described in Isaiah 28:16?

Chapter 10

THE NEED OF THE JEWS TO HEAR THE GOSPEL MESSAGE
ROMANS 10:1–21

Introduction

IN THIS CHAPTER of Romans we begin exactly where the ninth chapter ended. I don't know why there is a break in chapters here, but there is. Usually, when we come to a new chapter we think, "Well, OK, a new line of thinking." Let's compare the first verses of the tenth chapter and the first verses of the ninth chapter.

First let's look at chapter 9. Romans 9:1–3 says, "I am telling the truth in Christ, I am not lying, my conscience testifies with me in the Holy Spirit, that I have great sorrow and unceasing grief in my heart. For I could wish that I myself were accursed, separated from Christ for the sake of my brethren, my kinsmen according to the flesh…" He seems to be saying, "I would be willing to go to hell if it meant my fellow Jews would go to heaven." I don't know if I will ever be at that point—to be accursed, cut off from Christ if that would mean my kinsmen would be saved. That is a big step.

Next let's look at chapter 10. The first two verses deal with the same topic, the salvation of the Jews.

The Great Compassion Paul has for his Kin

Romans 10:1–10

Romans 10:1–2: "Brethren, my heart's desire and my prayer to God for them is for their salvation. For I bear them witness that they have a zeal for God, but not in accordance with knowledge." That must have been a slap in the face, because the Jewish people felt that they were the only ones who knew anything about God. In a sense they were right, for they were selected by God as custodians of the Law, and they were steeped in the Law. The Law was pure, holy, good, and perfect. While they had this tremendous background, they didn't understand that the Law also was an escort or a tutor (Galatians 3:24). The Law was a tutor that was to lead them and escort them to Christ. The Jews' lack of knowledge is seen here. Verse 3: "For not knowing about God's righteousness…" That is the Gospel, which is the power of God unto Salvation, for therein is revealed the righteousness of God (Romans 1:16). Romans 3:21–22 says, "But now apart from the Law the righteousness of God has been manifested, being witnessed by the Law and the Prophets, even the righteousness of God through faith in Jesus Christ for all those who believe; for there is no distinction…" The righteousness of God has been manifested. The Law and the Prophets bore witness of it, and the Jews knew that. But even though they knew it, they did not come to acknowledge it. They were aware of the coming of that manifestation, and yet they were ignorant as to its accomplishment. It was accomplished in the person of Christ. Now they shouldn't have been ignorant, but they were. This is what Paul is saying here.

"For not knowing about God's righteousness and seeking to establish their own…" (verse 3). They sought to establish their own righteousness through a Law that was good, holy, perfect, and righteous. That was the trouble! They could not fulfill the demands of the Law, and God, being just, would have to enact a punishment according to the Law. The Law became to them a means of condemnation rather than salvation. Not that the Law was weak but that man was weak in the flesh and could not adhere to it. Verse 3 continues, "…they did not subject themselves to the righteousness of God." That righteousness is vested in the person of Jesus Christ.

Romans 10:4 "For Christ is the end of the law for righteousness…" Or the goal of the Law for righteousness "…to everyone who believes." What then is the basic difference seen here? Jesus is good, perfect, holy, righteous, and just. The Law is also good, perfect, holy, righteous, and just. How is it then that one leads to death and the other leads to life? Well, the Law leads to death in that man can't meet its demands, man cannot fulfill it; but here is Christ, on this other hand, to lead us to life. This is why it is so important to have an incarnate God—that is to have God come in the flesh and come under the Law. For when God came in the flesh, He fulfilled the righteousness of the Law, the holiness of the Law, the perfection of the Law. John 1:14 says, "And the Word became flesh and dwelt among us and we beheld His glory, glory as of the only begotten from the Father full of grace and truth."

Since Jesus was conceived by the Holy Spirit with a seed that had no sin inherent within it, there was neither physical death nor spiritual death in Him so that Jesus was freed from death. That is good. But what does that have to do with me? Here is where grace comes in. Oh, man, does it ever! For this good, righteous, perfect, holy man who completed every tenet of the Law, death was not there. Yet God sent His own Son to die for the ungodly so that our penalty was assumed by Him (Romans 5:8). As that penalty was assumed by Him, we can wrap around us His righteousness. Galatians 3:27 states, "For all of you who were baptized into Christ have clothed yourselves with Christ." What and who God sees in us on the Day of Judgment is "Christ in me my hope of Glory" (Col. 1:27). That is the difference. Through the righteousness of God and the grace of God, He has assumed our debt. This was what the Jews did not believe or accept.

Romans 10:5: "For Moses writes that the man who practices the righteousness which is based on law shall live by that righteousness." But they couldn't do it! We tried going through the Ten Commandments previously and found that we failed miserably—20% at the highest, and that was it! Verse 6–7: "But the righteousness based on faith speaks as follows: '*Do not say in your heart, "who will ascend into heaven?"* (that is, to bring Christ down), or *"who will descend into the abyss?"* (that is, to bring Christ up from the dead).'" What in the world is going on here anyway? Let me share with you what I think, in my humble opinion, Paul is saying. I will put this spin on it, and you may have another idea; but I am quite comfortable with this, even though it is a little different. My understanding is, not by our work can we bring down from Heaven our justification, for no man can bring Christ down out of heaven, and no man can bring Him up out of the earth. We just don't have that kind of power. This is God's doing. This is fundamental to our redemption, that Christ came down and He tasted of our hell (1 Peter 3:18–20). This is the act of God, not man. There is work in bringing our salvation. It is God's work, not man's work. It is the work of faith, the work of grace, the work of God. It is a work that we could not perform ourselves; only God could do it.

Romans 10:8: "But what does it say? '*The word is near you, in your mouth and in your heart*'—that is, the word of faith which we are preaching…" Paul is saying that this is the message that is near you. This is the message of faith. This is the message of divine intervention. This is the message of grace. He is starting to wind up all that he has been teaching. Verse 9: "…that if you confess with your mouth Jesus as Lord, and believe in your heart that God raised Him from the dead, you shall be saved…" Now notice that the confession is of the lordship of Jesus. We usually have people confess in the Savior, don't we? That is the frosting on the cake. He is the Savior. But as discussed before, to my knowledge, wherever the words "Savior" and "Lord" are used together, "Lord" always precedes "Savior." It is never "Savior and Lord," is it? It is always "Lord and Savior." You see, the saving ability of God comes at the price that we pay to accept His lordship. Once we have accepted His lordship, all of those things in our character that shouldn't be there we surrender unto the Lord Jesus. I want the Lord Jesus to lead, guide, and direct my life. I am here for a purpose. *Lord Jesus, show me that purpose, and lead me and guide me each step of each day.*

Let's look back in verse 9: "…that God raised Him from the dead…" That folds right back to the going into the abyss He raised Him up from. God did that! "…you will be saved…"

Once we have surrendered to the lordship of Jesus, it is unto, toward, or for salvation. We are on the right road. Verse 10: "…for with the heart man believes resulting in righteousness …" This believing results in righteousness. I have a little asterisk by that word "resulting"—a resulting to righteousness. In the King James translation it has the word "unto." I like that translation—"unto" or resulting in. It is an "unto" step. We are getting closer toward salvation, as it were, resulting in or unto righteousness. Verse 10 continues, "…and with the mouth he confesses, resulting in salvation." Once the heart has been surrendered to the lordship of Jesus, we make the confession, whether it is inwardly or outwardly or both. It is that confession that is within the depths of our hearts—that God raised Him from the dead—and it will result in our salvation.

QUESITONS AND DISCUSSION FOR THE GREAT COMPASSION PAUL HAS FOR HIS KIN

1. Paul's heart's desire and prayer is for whom? (See verse 1.)

2. What did the Jews lack? _____ What did they have? _____ (See verse 2.)

3. What specific knowledge did they lack? (See verse 3.)

4. How is the goal for finding Righteousness obtained? (See verses 3–5.)

5. The righteousness of the Law is _____ (verse 5).

6. The righteousness of God is based up on the work of _____ (verse 6).

7. What work was that which is outside the ability of man? (See verses 6–7.)

8. The message of righteousness is _____ you in your _____ and _____ _____ (verse 8).

9. The two points we are to confess are? (See verse 9.)

10. With the heart we _____ with the mouth _____ (verse 10).

Both Jew and Gentile Have the Same Witness to Heed

Romans 10:11–21

Romans 10:11: "For the Scripture says, '*whoever believes in him will not be disappointed.*'" No matter how distressful or miserable or negative circumstances that surround us may become, we have been granted peace and joy that flood our hearts, transcend our earthly problems, and pass all understanding. Because of that (among other things), we will not be disappointed by our faith. Paul states that our struggles are counted as dung (waste) compared to the excellencies of the knowledge of Him (Philippians 3:7).

Romans 10:12: "For there is no distinction between Jew and Greek…" Now neither party to which this book is addressed (Jews or Romans) is going to like this. The Jews are not going to be favorable toward this, and from a military or human domain standpoint, the Romans certainly are not going to count the Jews as being equal. The Jews are not equal to the Romans, for the Jews live over in that land that is the armpit of the Roman Empire. Here, Paul says there is no distinction. How can Jew and Greek be considered equal? Let's look at the rest of verse 12: "…for the same Lord is Lord of all, abounding in riches for all who call on Him…" Since all have the same Lord, all can come to that Lord, and there is no distinction in the manner in which they come to Him. It is uniform.

Romans 10:13–14: "…for '*whoever will call on the name of the lord will be saved.*' How then shall they call upon Him in whom they have not believed? And how shall they believe in Him whom they have not heard? And how shall they hear without a preacher?" It is impossible to believe on anything for which there has been no testimony. A person who has never seen a light switch cannot turn on a light until he or she witnesses or is told how the light is turned on. There is no faith without testimony, secularly or religiously. All people live by faith. The question is what is the object of that faith? Verses 15–17 fully develop this premise: "And how shall they preach unless they are sent? Just as it is written, '*how beautiful are the feet of those who bring good news of good things!*' However, they did not all heed the good news; for Isaiah says, '*lord, who has believed our report?*' So faith comes from hearing, and hearing by the word of Christ." Look back at the circle regarding saving faith in Chapter 4. This circle shows the properties of faith. I am extremely comfortable with what is illustrated in the circle of saving faith. I feel as though when all the scriptures regarding salvation are tied together in a package, this shows the only justifiable conclusion for our obtaining a saving relationship with God.

Romans 10:18: "But I say, surely they have never heard, have they? Indeed they have…" Next Paul quotes some different Old Testament passages where the Jews have been witnessed to. The first quote is in the second half of verse 18, "…*their voice has gone out into all the earth, and their words to the ends of the world.*" They cannot plead ignorance. The next quote is found in the next verse (19): "But I say, surely Israel did not know, did they? First Moses says,

'I will make you jealous by that which is not a nation, by a nation without understanding will I anger you.'" Now this verse was reassuring to the Roman hearers. Yet there is another quote in verse 20: "And Isaiah is very bold and says, '*I was found by those who did not seek me, I became manifest to those who did not ask for me.*'" That is referring to the Gentiles. The last quote is in verse 21: "But as for Israel He says, '*all the day long I have stretched out my hands to a disobedient and obstinate people.*'" You see, the key from a divine standpoint is grace and from a human standpoint is faith. Are we saved by faith alone? When you understand what constitutes faith and the properties of faith, there's absolutely no question about it.

QUESTIONS AND DISCUSSION FOR BOTH JEW AND GENTILE HAVE THE SAME WITNESS TO HEED

1. Those who believe will not be _____ (verse 11).

2. When we call, regardless of who we are, we all abound in _____ (verse 12).

3. The three steps needed for us to call on Him are _____ (verse 14).

4. Heeding what we _____ so we may obtain _____ (verses 16–17).

5. The three sources who related the glad tidings are _____ _____.

THE RELATIONSHIP OF GOD TO THE JEWS AND THE GENTILES
ROMANS 11:1–36

Introduction

THIS CHAPTER CONCLUDES the teaching phase of Paul's letter. Let's pause a moment and review what we learned in the first ten chapters. The first part of Romans describes the means and way of salvation by first establishing the universal need. The first two chapters explain that this universal need was met by the righteousness of God that induces faith as manifested in Jesus Christ. Through that faith and that righteousness, we can find justification, not through the performance of deeds or the Law, but through the reliance upon the righteousness of God that is poured out by His grace. This faith is reemphasized in the fourth chapter, basically using Abraham as the model for us to emulate in our faith.

We noted in chapters 5–7 that Paul talks about the grace of God, when it came, and how it is superior to the advent of sin through Adam. We find this in the latter part of the fifth chapter, along with the concept that grace supersedes that which Adam incurred. We should not take advantage of that grace, as is says in the sixth chapter, "What shall we say then, shall we continue in sin that grace may abound? God forbid!" Why don't we realize that as we were immersed into Christ, we were immersed into His death, into His burial, and into His resurrection? Even as Christ was raised from the dead, so also we can walk in a new life. The involuntary shackles of sin that held us in Satan's sway now have been broken, and with those fetters loose, we want, long, yearn, desire to find a voluntary servitude under the lordship of Jesus Christ. In this servitude we can cast away this worry of involuntary bondage to sin. Romans 7:14–26 describes the terrible dilemma that we are in when under the involuntary servitude of sin. We find ourselves compelled to violate our desires. I want to do right, but I don't; what I don't want to do and hate, I do. This leads us to say, "Boy, oh boy, oh wretched man that I am!" But

Romans goes on to show that we now can fully appreciate knowing that our sins have been swallowed up in the righteousness of Jesus and that we have victory in Christ. That victory is assured to us because of the working and the presence of the Holy Spirit in our lives.

The eighth chapter of Romans was devoted to the working and the presence of the Holy Spirit in our lives. It concludes with a marvelous declaration that there is nothing external or internal that will be able to separate us from the love of God that we find in Christ Jesus.

Is this, then, on an equal basis? What about those who were the chosen seed? Can there also be an equality of all people, regardless of their heritage or their longevity, regardless of their place and position in the Lord? Can there be equality within the great grace of God and within the realm of His loving kindness? In the ninth through the eleventh chapters of Romans, Paul answers this question.

We saw in the ninth chapter that Paul had a very strong burden for the people of Israel, who had ushered and escorted the human race up to the Christ. After doing this arduous task of escorting, they as a people cut themselves off from God by rejecting Jesus as the Christ. They did not recognize their need of the New Covenant of Grace.

In the tenth chapter, we found that Paul reiterated the theme of Romans by saying, "Brethren my heart's desire and supplication is for them that they may be saved." Then he shares with us some of the fundamental principles by which a person can be ushered into this New Covenant: Faith has to be based upon knowledge; knowledge has to be imparted through the Word of God. The Word of God will not be imparted unless there is somebody to impart it to. There will be no one to impart that Word unless they are sent. It is the responsibility of the local group to retain a minister and to identify missionaries and to send them on their way. We observed this in Romans 10:14.

I'd like to back that up one step, not to say that that should not be done or should not be equated to the intent of this scripture. But I think that the most dynamic personalities in Christendom, in spite of the organization that they may have been affiliated with, are people who feel as though they had a call from God, not in a physical vision or manifestation, but in the prompting of their hearts and their souls. They are so motivated by that call that they will not be deterred from the ministry that they feel the Lord has sent to them. No matter how we may look at an organization, including a church organization, and feel as though there is a great deal of corruption in it, there are people like Mother Theresa who rise, not because of the organization, but in spite of it. She was motivated to the extent that she counted it no sacrifice at all to do what she did.

I think the great evangelists of the past and present would feel much the same, regardless of whether or not we concur with all of their theology. I heard a statement attributed to Dwight L. Moody that, "The world has yet to see a fully committed man, save Jesus," and he was striving to arrive at that level of commitment. Like Paul, he said, "I press on toward the goal, but I haven't reached it yet" (Col. 1:27, paraphrased). Billy Graham would be another good example of this type of believer. Men like Billy Graham and Dwight L. Moody have kept their motives straight and have not been blinded by wine, women, or money. They have made their pleas, and their lives are very sacred vessels to the proclamation of their ministry as they understood it.

Such can be said, too, of some in the Restoration movement, which began in the early 1800s. Thomas and Alexander Campbell, father and son, became absolutely obsessed with freeing the church from the entanglements of the European denominational encroachment that was made upon people. It was those encroachments that drove the very first white settlers to America and in the wake of the Revolutionary War. They wanted the church to have the same freedom that our nation now has. In that obsession and devotion, they were willing to focus their whole lives toward the goal of a unity of all believers in Christ outside of denominational partitions.

It is going to take the same kind of passion within the pulpits, within the leadership, and within the congregations of churches today to find out where people will be called. It is those called ones that need to ascend to the top in order that the lost might be saved. May this be said of us, "How beautiful are the feet of those who bring good news of good things" (Romans 10:15). Notice the very positive word selection: "good news" and "good things."

Now we will end our review with the last verse of chapter 10. Paul writes, "But as for Israel He (Isaiah) says, *all the day long I have stretched out my hands to a disobedient and obstinate people*" (Isa. 65:2). That is how chapter 10 closes. It's not very attractive is it? After such a hopeful note, we discover that the principles do not always fall upon the ears of those who should be the most receptive and most retentive of them.

Has God Rejected His People?

Romans 11:1–10

Romans 11:1: "I say then, God has not rejected His people, has He? May it never be!" It is not God who rejects; it is we who reject. And we need to get the subject and the object in the correct sequence. So Paul says, "May it never be!" Verse 1 continues, "For I too am an Israelite, a descendant of Abraham, of the tribe of Benjamin."

Let me just deviate here and throw in a little trivia. Do you remember who David's real buddy was before he became the king? Jonathan. Jonathan was of the tribe of Benjamin. The Benjaminites were the tribe that was basically left-handed. Benjamin and Judah, along with most of the Levites, were the only tribes left after the division of Israel. Ten tribes went into oblivion because they rejected the word, message, and principles of God. This left two. Then Jonathan and David became close friends. David was of the tribe of Judah, Jonathan of the tribe of Benjamin. They made a covenant one with another that Jonathan would be the servant of David. In principle, this covenant was going to be an everlasting covenant. Of course, it couldn't be everlasting in material things. As a result, the tribe of Benjamin became subservient to the tribe of Judah.

Now, who in all of the New Testament wrote the most books; walked the most miles; preached the most sermons; endured the most hardships; and was jailed, stoned, and shipwrecked? Paul, a Benjaminite, was fulfilling that old prophecy of being subservient to the King of Kings and the Lord of Lords, who was of the tribe of Judah. That is just a little bit of trivia that you can associate with all the way through the Bible. The Bible has so many of these little patterns that just develop, and as you see them, it gives a little thrill to appreciate that this book is so beautifully and wondrously written.

Paul's logical and chronological events in all of his books are just fantastic. I hope that we have seen so far in this book of Romans a little bit of that logical and orderly development—step by step by step—and now he is closing with these steps of establishing the need and means for a relationship with God. He lays down a premise and then develops it, which leads to another premise, which he also develops. That premise is not isolated from the former, but it is interlinked. So we can see all through this book that kind of development. It is really exciting!

Romans 11:2–5: "God has not rejected His people whom He foreknew. Or do you not know what the Scripture says in the passage about Elijah, how he pleads with God against Israel? 'Lord, *they have killed your prophets, they have torn down your altars, and I alone am left, and they are seeking my life.*' But what is the divine response to him? '*I have kept* for Myself *seven thousand men who have not bowed the knee to baal.*' In the same way then, there has also come to be at the present time a remnant according to God's gracious choice." Not all of Israel was rejected. Just a part of Israel did not find a place in God's plan of redemption, because they rejected that plan. It was not God rejecting them, as we have already pointed out.

Romans 11:6: "But if it is by grace, it is no longer on the basis of works; otherwise grace is no longer grace." This is a strong verse. You might want to underline it. If grace was the result of works, it would be payment that was due to us—something that we earned. This was the great failure of the people of Israel concerning the Law: they could not maintain the works of the Law and hence, they fell under the penalty of the Law. Under that penalty there needed to be a justification for their deeds and a means by which they could have access again to a relationship with God. Justification for their works was done by Christ at the cross. Grace took works to bring it into being, but not the works of man. It is in Christ's work that we then place our trust. A noted orator of the 19th century said, "On a life I did not live, on a death I did not die, I place my trust for eternity." That pretty much sums it up.

Romans 11:7: "What then? What Israel is seeking, it has not obtained, but those who were chosen obtained it, and the rest were hardened…" They obtained it by faith and hence were chosen. They rejected it by faithlessness and hence were hardened. There is an Old Testament scripture given in verses 8–10 that substantiates that premise: "…just as it is written, '*god gave them a spirit of stupor, eyes to see not and ears to hear not, down to this very day.' And David says, 'let their table become a snare and a trap, and a stumbling block and a retribution to them. Let their eyes be darkened to see not, and bend their backs forever'"* (NASB).

QUESTIONS AND DISCUSSION FOR HAS GOD REJECTED HIS PEOPLE?

1. Explain how God did not forsake His people (verse 1).

2 What is the difference between foreknowledge and foreordination? (See verse 2.)

3. What is the similarity of the remnant of Jewish Christians to the times of Elijah? (See verses 2–4.)

4. When would grace no longer become grace? (See verse 6.)

The Message to the Gentiles and the Restoration of Israel

Romans 11:11–32

Romans 11:11: "I say then, they did not stumble so as to fall, did they? May it never be! But by their transgression salvation has come to the Gentiles, to make them jealous." That is a hard one. Let's try this on for size. They fell, not because God pushed them but because they were not responsive to God. Now their fall became the richness for the Gentiles. Had they not fallen by the hardness of their hearts there would have been no crucifixion. Does that make some sense? If the Jews had not turned and hardened their hearts, there would have been no crucifixion. The fact that they were hardened opened a way and an avenue for the remission, not only of their transgressions, but also of the transgressions of all people. This means that now the family of God is not to be vested within a single human race, but it is to be vested in all people who by faith choose Jesus Christ. Then all who accept Christ become the chosen people of God. Verse 11 said, "...to make them jealous." You see, the thing that bothered the Jewish Christians the most in the early church was that Gentiles, who did not have a Jewish legacy, were being accepted as Christians anyway. They hadn't paid their dues. The Jews were jealous over the fact that these Gentiles, who would not have come through Judaism, would not have followed the rites of the Law, and did not have the seal of the Jew through circumcision, would then be allowed to be a part of the family of God. As Christians, the Gentiles did become a part of God's family.

That the Gentiles were Christians is evident in the manner in which they loved one another; they took care of one another and they propagated their message. The Jews never did propagate their message. They were a cloistered group, were isolated, and were introverted within themselves. Israel had very little desire to spread Judaism. If Gentiles came and wanted to accept Judaism, then that was their desire, but it came from no overt action on the part of the Jews. The Jews today have laws in Israel that forbid people to proselytize. It is just foreign to their country. Laws don't always stop the progress of the Gospel though, and this is seen everywhere. As a matter of fact, there are many Christian Jews in Israel today.

On one of our trips to the Holy Land, we had an opportunity to go to an underground Bible study with the Jewish Christians. It was in a home, and it was fascinating. We snuck out of the hotel by night. The study was in the hotel clerk's home, and she took me there. We had a study, and then I had to sneak back into the hotel at night. I don't think I would do that today, but it was fun then. Most of the Christian missions in Jerusalem are by nature Arabic, and boy, are they needed! "Now if their transgression is riches for the world and their failure is riches for the Gentiles, how much more will their fulfillment be!" (verse 12).

Romans 11:13: "But I am speaking to you who are Gentile…" Oh, let's perk up our ears! Here we go…"…Inasmuch then as I am an apostle…" Paul is the "sent one" or apostle because he was called by God and sent by the church in Antioch. "…of Gentiles, I magnify my ministry…" He was not magnifying himself, he was magnifying his ministry. Verse 14: "…if somehow I might move to jealousy my fellow countrymen and save some of them." Paul thought that if others had to get mad at him in order to reach a premise then, hey, that was OK, as long as they were brought into a closer and more complete relationship with God. Verse 15: "For if their rejection is the reconciliation of the world, what will their acceptance be but life from the dead?" Their rejection brought about a reconciliation of the world. If they would be converted, it indeed would be life from the dead. Now, that phrase doesn't go over well, because that phrase implies that they are dead. They were dead in their trespasses and in their sins. Later on we will find that they have even been sawed off from the tree of God.

Romans 11:16–17: "If the first piece of dough is holy, the lump is also; and if the root is holy, the branches are too. But if some of the branches were broken off, and you, being a wild olive, were grafted in among them and became partaker with them of the rich root of the olive tree…" The "wild olive" refers to the Gentiles. The "rich root" is seen in the person of Jesus. Verse 18: "…do not be arrogant toward the branches; but if you are arrogant, remember that it is not you who supports the root, but the root supports you." Remember where our strength comes from. This is indeed the position that we need to appreciate. Verses 19–20: "You will say then, 'Branches were broken off so that I might be grafted in.' Quite right, they were broken off for their unbelief, but you stand by your faith. Do not be conceited, but fear…" You stand in your faith. They were broken off in their faithlessness. So it is faith that makes the difference. Verse 21 "…for if God did not spare the natural branches, He will not spare you, either." So keep the faith, hang on to the faith, and cherish the faith. For it is only through faith that we receive the nourishment from the root. The osmoses process from the dynamics of Jesus Christ is absorbed into our character and into our spirit.

Verse 22: "Behold then the kindness and severity of God; to those who fell, severity, but to you, God's kindness, if you continue in His kindness; otherwise you also will be cut off." I just don't know how you can support the concept of once in grace always in grace and accept this passage of Scripture. For there is nothing external or internal that can separate us, save our faith. It took faith to obtain grace. If we lose or abuse that faith, then just like Israel was cut off, so too shall we. Verses 23–24: "And they also, if they do not continue in their unbelief, will be grafted in, for God is able to graft them in again. For if you were cut off from what is by nature a wild olive tree, and were grafted contrary to nature into a cultivated olive tree, how much more will these who are the natural branches be grafted into their own olive tree?" Boy, weren't we a pretty wild vine? I don't even want to go there. I want to stay as far away from that as possible. When we were a wild olive branch He took us who were contrary to His will, brought us in, and grafted us into the family tree of God. Then most assuredly the natural olive branch, which has been severed by faithlessness, can more easily be grafted back into that natural plan in which God wanted them to live and be.

Romans 11:25: "For I do not want you, brethren, to be uninformed of this mystery—so that you will not be wise in your own estimation—that a partial hardening has happened to Israel until the fullness of the Gentiles has come in…" I don't think that we are anywhere near to the fullness of the Gentiles coming in. Only a miniscule percentage of the Gentile population claims to be Christian. Even then, only a smaller percentage of that number has really adopted these principles and applied them to their everyday lives in their society within the family of God and within the society of the world. I think we have a lot of growing up to do. But God reads hearts; I just see manifestations, and God sees much more than I do. He is willing and able to assimilate everyone who calls on Him.

Romans 11:26–28: "…and so all Israel will be saved; just as it is written, '*the deliverer will come from zion, he will remove ungodliness from jacob. This is my covenant with them, when I take away their sins.*' From the standpoint of the gospel they are enemies for your sake, but from the standpoint of God's choice they are beloved for the sake of the fathers…" God still has a great compassion for Israel and for the Israelites. Even though they have denounced Him, there is still a great compassion that God has for them. God has an ability to love the unlovely. Aren't you glad for that? If you want to adapt this to the world situation (and I am always a little scared to do that because we can get off on some real tangents), God does have a soft spot in His heart for Israel, even though to this day they are rejecting Him. It is ironic that those who rejected the Christ, and still reject Him today, are dependent upon those who have accepted the Christ for their very longevity and well-being. That is in God's plan. So who is the servant of whom? Let us not become arrogant. Remember, we are still the wild olive branch that has been grafted in by God's grace. We need to utilize this posture in every way that we can to enrich, encourage, and embolden one another in our service to the Lord.

Romans 11:29: "…for the gifts and the calling of God are irrevocable." I love the way this portion of the book concludes. When God grants a gift, He does not take it back. We may desert it, but He will not issue a recall. God does not vacillate. What He does, He does, and it is irrevocable. Verse 30: "For just as you once were disobedient to God, but now have been shown mercy because of their disobedience…" Even though we have vacillated and been inconsistent through our disobedience, God will still show mercy. Verse 31: "…so these also now have been disobedient, in order that because of the mercy shown to you they also may now be shown mercy." Our having been grafted in by the mercy of God gives a vivid illustration that God will also show mercy to Jews, the severed natural olive branches. Verse 32: "For God has shut up all in disobedience so that He may show mercy to all." For all disobedience should cause all of us, wild or natural, to appreciate the might of His mercy.

QUESTIONS AND DISCUSSION FOR THE MESSAGE TO THE GENTILES AND THE RESTORATION OF ISRAEL

1. What were the two results of the Jewish leaders rejecting Christ? (See verse 11.)

2. What is the reason given for the Gentiles obtaining salvation? (See verse 11.)

3. Name the two types of olive branches and what they illustrate (verses 17–21).

4. Which were cut off and why? (See verses 15–17.)

5. Which were grafted in and why? (See verses 19–20.)

6. How and when can the cut off branches again be grafted in? (See verses 22–24.)

7. Could the wild branch be cut off once it is grafted in? (See verse 21.)

8. From what standpoint are the Jews enemies of God? (See verse 28.)

9. Why are the Jews still the beloved of God? (See verses 28–29.)

10. How has God shut up all in disobedience? (See verse 29.)

Great Praise Given to God

Romans 11:33–36

Romans 11:33: "Oh, the depth of the riches both of the wisdom and knowledge of God! How unsearchable are His judgments and unfathomable His ways!" Here, Paul, this great thinker, has tied the redemption of Israel and the Gentiles together within God's family. They are all the children, and hence, the people of God. All have the same means of obtaining God's redemption— accepting by faith the grace that God has offered. This is just barely plowing the crust of the ground. We haven't gotten down into the deep furrow of the rich soil as yet. Oh brethren, the richness and the wisdom and the knowledge of God are beyond human comprehension! Verse 34: "For *who has known the mind of the lord, or who became his counselor?*'" You know, sometimes we feel as though we have to tell God what to do. In some unbeknownst and mysterious way to me, being humble as I am, I don't know why God hasn't sought my council as yet; but He hasn't (said tongue-in-cheek). Verses 35–36: "Or *who has first given to him that it might be paid back to him again?*' for from Him and through Him and to Him are all things. To Him be the glory forever. Amen." So ends the theology of the book of Romans.

But we are not at the end yet. In chapters 12 through 15 Paul responds to the question: What is going to be our response to this great action of redemption? By displaying the righteousness of God we obtained through faith given by grace, we are victorious by the advent of His Holy Spirit. So knowing that we are a part of the family of God, what is going to be our response? The very first thing Paul says regarding our response is seen in the opening of the twelfth chapter.

QUESTIONS AND DISCUSSION FOR GREAT PRAISE GIVEN TO GOD

1. Discuss the greatness of God (verses 33–35).

2. Discuss His great eternal glory (verse 36).

APPLICATIONS OF PRINCIPLES TAUGHT

ROMANS 12:1–21

Introduction

THIS TWELFTH CHAPTER of Romans is one that is so challenging. The first eleven chapters were basically teaching chapters sprinkled with some preaching. The last five chapters are basically preaching chapters, the application of the previous teaching. (Teaching is the sharing of information, and preaching is the applying of that information.) This application begins in chapter twelve.

Appeals Made in Response to God's Mercies

Romans 12:1–2

The twelfth chapter of Romans speaks of these four categories: our relationship with God, our relationship with self, our relationship with things, and our relationship with others. The first two verses deal with our relationship with God.

Paul starts by begging, pleading, beseeching—willing to get down on hands and knees, really pouring out his heart. Romans 12:1: "Therefore I urge you, brethren by the mercies of God…" These mercies are the revelation of His righteousness in Jesus Christ through His power unto salvation, which we all need. Even when we don't think it is possible, this power can be reached by faith. Faith, following His directions and placing our lives in His trusting hands, does work. His will will be accomplished. And this faith results in the grace of God being poured out upon us. As we join Jesus in His death, burial, and resurrection, God's grace liberates us from involuntary servitude and the slavery of Satan's grip. Our failures are now in the past, because our victory is in Christ Jesus. This victory is confirmed by the presence of the

Holy Spirit. The Holy Spirit bears witness that we are the children of God, intercedes for us in prayer, and assures us there is nothing upon earth—physical, temporal, or spiritual—that can separate us from the love of God.

Those of us who are Gentiles have been grafted as natural branches into that olive tree of peace. That grafting makes us heirs, joint heirs of the kingdom with Jesus Christ. This act of grace identifies the key mercies of our redemption and reconciliation. God, by His grace and powerful hand, firmly cementing our ability to have a relationship with Him. Paul says he has a right to plead with us because of these mercies.

Paul continues and explains what he wants us to do as far as our physical bodies are concerned (verse1): "...to present your bodies a living and holy sacrifice, acceptable to God, which is your spiritual service of worship." A living sacrifice is, in light of His mercy, a reasonable request. That we choose to commit our lives without reservation to the purpose Jesus has called us is the call Paul asks us to answer. We need to use the talents we have without expectation of monetary reward or human acclaim, simply because we feel so grateful to God. We cannot gain entrance into heaven under the principles of the Law, for we have only gained that by the works of Christ. Grace has so touched our hearts that we can do nothing less than be completely in full service to Him. We dedicate our vocations to Him to use as a witnessing forum. The monetary income that we receive we dedicate to Him, using these funds as God's gift to sustain ourselves, to help our fellow man, and to expand His kingdom. Self is crucified, and service is revived.

Thus, we are set apart from the world. Verse 2 says, "And do not be conformed to this world, but be transformed by the renewing of your mind, so that you may prove what the will of God is, that which is good and acceptable and perfect." We may only conform ourselves to the world to the extent that the world has conformed itself to the principles of Christ. But where the world has not conformed itself to the principles as articulated in the Scriptures, we will not follow. When we get to the thirteenth chapter we are going to have a struggle with this. Just keep that in mind until we get there.

Relationships

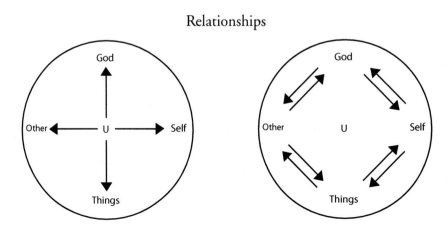

APPLICATIONS OF PRINCIPLES TAUGHT

Think of Self: Things you think about yourself, a good or poor image.

Think of Others: Poor relationship with self produces poor relationships with others. Good relationship with self produces good relationships with others.

Think of Things: Things are tools we use, not a master that we serve. Our responsibility is for good stewardship.

Think of God: Our relationship with God is to realize our flaws and, being kissed by God's grace, to realize our value.

The two circle diagrams above show various personal relationships. You are in the middle, with God, Self, Things, and Other(s) on the four sides. Your position is not a stationary position, for sometimes you are very close in your relationship with each one of these four categories: Sometimes you drift very close to things, and other times you drift close to others and are occupied with them. Sometimes you drift very close to self and are involved in matters that only pertain to you. Other times you are on a spiritual high and are in very close relationship to, conversation with, worship of, and praise to God. These other relationships are not broken, but they are stretched because we are closest to one of the four. It is like you are on a rubber band—the closer you get to one, the further you are from the others.

The key to meaningful relationships is our relationship with God. If you are in a good relationship with God, you will not be self-centered, egotistical, or boastful. Nor will you be self-effacing or down on yourself with an "I can't do it" attitude. You will realize you are a child of God in spite of your weaknesses. You will live a victorious life because you have been kissed by His grace. Then, when you are in good relationship with yourself, because of your relationship with God, you can have good relationships with others. We are to love our neighbors as we love ourselves (Matthew 22:39; Mark 12:31; Luke 10:27). (There are some people who are so down on themselves that I wouldn't want them to be my neighbors.) You will love and treat your neighbor even as Christ loves and treats you. If you have a relationship with God, seeking first His kingdom, you will realize that all the "things" are supplied by Him to be of service to you. The question that many of us need to address here is: Do things serve me or do I serve the things I have? Are things my master or my servant? So do you see that all of these categories are enhanced by our relationship with God and hence that makes our entire life beautiful? God is the key to successful relationships with ourselves, with others, and with things, as the second diagram endeavors to illustrate.

As mentioned before, the first two verses of this chapter are about our relationships resulting from the mercies of God; whether it is your relationship with yourself, with others, with things, or with God. The best of all of these relationships is predicated upon our relationship with God, which causes the relationship with God to be the most important.

Now remember, a relationship with God can only be accomplished by divine intervention, and so there has to be a transformation of our minds. This will involve a change of goals, aspirations, wants, and desires. Our whole mode of thinking is altered. We develop a hunger and thirst for His word, conversations with Him become precious times, and we have a longing to be with other Christians.

The word "transformed" in Romans 12:2 is the same word that is used in Matthew 17:2, where Jesus was transfigured and was seen in a spiritual entity rather than in the physical entity that His disciples were accustomed to seeing. This vision is again repeated in Revelation 1:13–16. There is only one other place in Scripture (2 Cor. 3:18) in which this word "transfiguration" or "transformed" (as we see it here) is used. It is the same basic Greek word. This spiritual transfiguration or transformation can only come because of our redemption by God's grace, because of the implementation of His Holy Spirit. The Holy Spirit allows us to have this great relationship with God. Our faith is required, but God's response is so much greater than our faith. It seems a cheap price to pay. Paul is asking us to respond by having this kind of relationship with God.

As mentioned before, our relationship with God will have a tremendous bearing upon how we feel about ourselves. How we feel about ourselves will have a tremendous bearing upon how we feel about others. "Love your neighbor as you love yourself." Sometimes I don't feel too good about myself. On those occasions I say, "Oh, Ted, why in the world did you do that dumb, stupid thing? What is the matter with you anyway?" Then I say to my neighbor, "How could you do that dumb, stupid thing? What is the matter with you anyway?" I just love my neighbor the way I love me. But there is a higher love spoken of in John 13:34. According to this, the New Commandment is to "Love your neighbor even as I have loved you." That is a constant that is the law of love in the New Covenant that we now live under. This type of love and our relationship with God helps us to see ourselves as the pride of all God's creation.

Consider Ephesians 2:10: "For we are His workmanship…" Oh yes we are, His poetry, His masterpiece. Just think of the vastness of all the universes and how we feel so proud of ourselves because we have landed a couple of tinker toys on Mars. With His finger God flung the stars out and made not only this universe but also all the cosmos. Man has not yet found one speck of life anywhere else in this universe except here upon this earth. Here is this tiny sphere in the midst of all of these billions of spheres, and only this one possesses life.

The only lives that are created in the image of God are human lives (Genesis 1:26–27). The only human lives that are reconciled and have a relationship with God are Christians, those who are of His family. You are an important person in the eyes of Almighty God. Bless the Lord, oh my soul! We can see ourselves like that, without getting puffed up, because it is only by God's grace. All glory and honor go to God, for that great, esteemed position belongs to Him. We should indeed view ourselves in all humility, with no false piety and with no sense of grandeur.

Consider the twelfth chapter of 2 Corinthians, where Paul is saying, essentially, I buffeted my weakness in my flesh, and I prayed a whole heap to get rid of it. It is still there, but I now know that God's grace is sufficient to aide me in my limitations and weaknesses. Then this great apostle says he is nothing. Like Paul, it is when we come to the place where we say, "I am nothing," that God can make something of our lives. This changes our attitudes toward others to the same attitude that God has towards us. If everyone were changed in this way, wouldn't that be a great world to live in? We could take all the locks off the doors!

QUESTIONS AND DISCUSSION FOR
APPEALS MADE IN RESPONSE TO GOD'S MERCIES

1. How is "service of worship" demonstrated? (See verse 1.)

2. Name two things that the "renewing of the mind" brings (verse 2).

The Formula for Service

Romans 12:3–8

Romans 12:3: "For through the grace given to me I say to everyone among you not to think more highly of himself than he ought to think; but to think so as to have sound judgment, as God has allotted to each a measure of faith." I just want to explore this measure of faith a little bit before Paul expands upon that concept. Did that mean that some have more faith in God than others? I don't know whether God is the object of faith here or not. All of us have different talents, and it is not wise to compare one against the other. This is not a competitive thing. The bottom line is God being glorified, His body being built-up, and people coming to the Lord. Some know how to sing and some know how to take the hand of a person who is in sorrow, hold that hand, and minister to that person just by being there. Yet others have strengths in other areas. So for this reason we must not think more highly of ourselves than we ought, because all that we have is of God.

Now let's see how Paul elaborates on verse three. Romans 12:4–8: "For just as we have many members in one body and all the members do not have the same function, so we, who are many, are one body in Christ, and individually members one of another. Since we have gifts that differ according to the grace given to us, each of us is to exercise them accordingly: if prophecy, according to the proportion of his faith; if service, in his serving; or he who teaches, in his teaching; or he who exhorts, in his exhortation; he who gives, with liberality; he who leads, with diligence; he who shows mercy, with cheerfulness." All of this has to do with a "you" relationship, the relationship that you (self) have with God.

QUESTIONS AND DISCUSSION FOR THE FORMULA FOR SERVICE

1. What has God allotted to us and how does it affect our self esteem? (See verse 3.)

2. What is the application to the illustration of our body? (See verses 4–5.)

3. Name seven gifts and how they are to be used (verses 6–8). Discuss each gift.

Our Relationship with Others and God

Romans 12:9–12

Paul now gets into a little bit of a different thing. It is now not only a "you" relationship, but also it is building to become a God relationship. Romans 12:9–12: "Let love be without hypocrisy. Abhor what is evil; cling to what is good. Be devoted to one another in brotherly love; give preference to one another in honor; not lagging behind in diligence, fervent in spirit, serving the Lord; rejoicing in hope, persevering in tribulation, devoted to prayer…" We are to be devoted to prayer, loving to pray. In order to fall in love with prayer, lean back, look out the window, and muse on the wonders of God. Allow the Scriptures to dance through your mind, picture the face of Christ, and allow His Word to flood through your soul. Oh, you will come out so refreshed! Start loving that time you have in conversation with God. The benefits include refreshment, insight, strength, direction, and peace.

QUESTIONS AND DISCUSSION FOR RELATIONSHIP
WITH GOD AND OTHERS

1. What is the key to good relationships? (See verse 9.)

2. Identify how love is manifested in our personalities (verses 9–12).

3. Name three qualities that demonstrate the will of God (verses 1–11).

4. Name ten mercies that God has demonstrated (verses 1–11).

Our Relationship with Others and Things

Romans 12:13–21

Romans 12:13: "…contributing to the needs of the saints…" Now Paul is building further and focusing on our relationships with our Christian brethren. We are to be devoted to one another, giving preference and honor to others above ourselves. There is a whole list of how we can do this and meet the needs of others. Verse 13: "…practicing hospitality." That is more than our responsibility; it is our opportunity to serve others. When serving others, we are served the same way by God. These are the tenets brought out in the first eleven chapters that are now applied to "others." God, by His mercies, is serving us so we have the privilege of serving others.

How are we going to react to others, especially to those of the world? Negative approaches aren't only found outside of the body of Christ. In Romans 12:14–15 Paul shows us how best to react to the negative actions of others. Verse 14: "Bless those who persecute you; bless and do not curse." We don't want to hear that. But there it is, calling us to do that which is exactly opposite of our natural yearnings. Verse 15: "Rejoice with those who rejoice, and weep with those who weep." Which of these do you think is easier to do?

Romans 12:16: "Be of the same mind toward one another; do not be haughty in mind…" Beware the attitude that says, "Look who I am. Look what I've done. Look where I've been. Look at my track record." Verse 16: "…but associate with the lowly." We are all one in Christ—no male, no female, no bondman, no slave, no freedman, and no difference. Don't forget the lowly. This is difficult to practice.

Let's say that one Sunday morning two visitors come to church. One drives up in a Mercedes. He's got rings on his fingers that nearly blind you; under the light they just sparkle. It's obvious he is extremely successful in the things of this world. The other guy appears to be homeless, or nearly so; you can't be sure, but he smells like the Lakers' Locker room after the championship game (or a hot barn on a hot summer day or a dumpster behind a meat packing plant or like he's been downwind of the sewage treatment plant or a combination of all of the above). The preacher encourages everyone to greet every visitor before leaving. To the visitors, he says, "If you don't shake hands with at least twenty people, come back next week, because I will have a sermon that will be a real barn-burner." What do we do? Who do you think would have the most greeters, Mr. Diamond or Mr. Dirty? Which one do you think needs the greatest help? Only God knows the answer to that one. Mr. Diamond can't get into heaven by his wealth. Mr. Dirty can't be kept out of heaven because of his hygiene. They both need to be kissed by God's grace.

My daughter taught me a valuable lesson. We learn a lot from our kids. Leanna, a missionary in Zimbabwe, was having a lot of hungry poor folk come to the gate of her home. Her daughters would come in and say, "There are beggars out there. What shall we do?"

Then Leanna would give them a packet of food and say, "Take this food and give it to them." This continued, and Leanna finally said, "I don't want you ever to call them beggars again."

"Well, what shall we call them then?" they asked.

Leanna said, "They are angels. For we minister to the angels unawares. They are angels." She now has about fifty angels. They became so crowded at her gate that they established a program connected with the church and obtained a social worker to take their names and document their credibility. Leanna takes funds out of her salary to buy food for her angels. Every week they get a food supplement. Isn't that something? There are so many stories I could tell, but I just shared that as an illustration about remembering the lowly.

Romans 12:16: "Do not be wise in your own estimation." Oh boy, that should hit almost every minister in the heart. It sure hits old Ted. Verses 17–18: "Never pay back evil for evil to anyone. Respect what is right in the sight of all men. If possible, so far as it depends on you, be at peace with all men." Sometimes it is not possible to be at peace with all men, but that must be because of their warfare and not because of ours. Because they want to inflict damage and hurt, we must be in a purely defensive mode. It is not that we must "conquer to destroy," we must "conquer to preserve."

Romans 12:19: "Never take your own revenge, beloved, but leave room for the wrath of God…" God is capable of doing His own work. Sometimes we try to take matters into our own hands. It's like we are saying, "Gee, God, how did you get along without me?" Verse 19: "…for it is written, *'vengeance is mine, I will repay,'* says the Lord." The 73rd Psalm is a great illustration of this. Asaph, the writer of this Psalm, is having a struggle. He acknowledges God and recognizes that God rewards those who have a pure heart; however, he is ready to slip. His feet are stumbling, and he has a problem. Here are all these wicked people, and they are living in splendor. Asaph is just barely making it as a poor choir leader. He was with a trio, and he also played the brass cymbals (1 Chronicles 15:17). He goes on and talks about this internal struggle. He looks at the world, and he looks at the wicked. He wonders, *How come I who have faith am living like this, and they, who have no faith, are living like that?* The end of Psalm 73 is beautiful. There is always a key verse in every Psalm that just leaps up at you and blesses your heart; Psalm 73:26 is such a verse. It says, "My flesh and my heart may fail, But God is the strength of my heart and my portion forever." Asaph comes to the conclusion that God is God and He will handle this matter. Like Asaph, sometimes we must go through a journey before we arrive at the right conclusion. Remember that God will deal with things in due time. He knows how to handle anything that comes our way. But just as it was for Asaph, patience and prayer are required of us as well.

Verses 20 and 21 relate how our relationship to things can be combined with our relationship with people. We need to put people ahead of things. Romans 12:20: *"But if your enemy is hungry, feed him, and if he is thirsty, give him a drink; for in so doing you will heap burning coals on his head."*

"Churchianity" can be cruel. I was in a church board meeting when I was preaching in Milwaukee, Oregon. I had this program that I knew would be a blessing, but there were some board members who were against it. This one particular lady was giving me opposition, and in the board meeting, I really lit into her. Bless her heart, she was embarrassed, and some of the board members were embarrassed too. I just scared the wits out of them, so they voted in the program. I felt great; I had gotten my way. But this great feeling of euphoria soon dimmed. The victory was at a great price, as I didn't know whether or not this lady would ever be back again. She had every right never to come back. If I'd been treated like that, I would never have gone back. I worried about it, thought about it, and didn't rest well that night.

The next day when I went out to get in my car, there was a beautiful chocolate pie with all the creamy stuff on it and a little note that said, "Ted, we love you." It was signed by her. Oh man, coals of fire, and I was burning. Even though the pie was delicious, it was a little like eating crow. I got home, showed my wife, Dorothy, and told her the story. She said, "Well, Ted, what are you going to do about it?" I got on the phone, called the lady, and asked if I could come over to see her. After arriving, we just cried together and prayed together, and rather than nurturing a fracture, she became one of our best friends. I learned one of the greatest lessons ever: People are more important than programs. Programs are peanuts, and people are pearls. We need to have these coals of fire heaped upon us now and again to humble us so that we (verse 21)—"Do not be overcome by evil, but overcome evil with good." Amen and amen.

QUESTIONS AND DISCUSSION FOR
RELATIONSHIP WITH OTHERS AND THINGS

1. Compare verse 13 with 1 John 3:11–16 and 4:7–11.

2. Do you have trouble complying with verse 14?

3. In verse 15, which do you feel is easier to do? Why?

4. How much do we discriminate, using the admonition of verse 16?

5. Is there room for improvement in your life when measured with the admonition of verses 17–20? Pick the area where you need to improve the most.

6. To be overcome or to be an overcomer depends on what? (See verse 17.)

7. How does verse 20 illustrate what you have and what others need?

8. Discuss the phrase "heap burning coals on his head."

Chapter 13

The Christian and Governments
Romans 13:1–14

Introduction

IN THIS CHAPTER we will find a shift of emphasis. Starting with our relationships with government, we are going to see the relationships with others stressed. Let's explore a Christian's opportunity and obligation in relation to governing authorities.

Our Relationship to the Principle of Governing

Romans 13:1–7

Romans 13:1: "Every person is to be in subjection to the governing authorities. For there is no authority except from God, and those which exist are established by God." The principle of governing has been ordained by God. However, the practice of how that principle is executed is determined by man. We know there are different forms of government: monarchy, dictatorship, republic, parliamentary, democratic, etc. We find differences between the governmental structure of the United States and that of most of the European countries. One can resist the practice of governing without resisting the principle of governing. The principle of governing is essential, because without any form of government there would be pure anarchy. There must be laws. God established the law, hence He ordained governing, the implementation of laws. Law and order, decency, respect, and honor are key elements within the society of man, and particularly within the Christian community. Man has a right to resist the type of government that is oppressive in order to provide a government that would be amicable with freedom and the outpouring of graciousness on behalf of society. This distinction needs to be made because often we feel that regardless of the type of government, we must be obedient to it. Government

127

needs to be formed and framed to be beneficial to the majority of the society being governed. Man must either obey government or move to reform it or leave.

In Matthew 22:15–22, Jesus set down a principle of subjecting ourselves to governmental authorities. He tells those questioning him about whether or not to pay taxes, "…render to Caesar the things that are Caesar's; and to God the things that are God's" (verse 21).

Romans 13:2: "Therefore whoever resists authority has opposed the ordinance of God…" God has ordained that we should be governed: "…and they who have opposed will receive condemnation upon themselves." If we feel as though we are a government unto ourselves, without obligation to society, then we find ourselves in a whole heap of trouble. Verse 3 talks of the responsibility of the citizen and the rulers. It says, "For rulers are not a cause of fear for good behavior, but for evil. Do you want to have no fear of authority? Do what is good and you will have praise from the same…" This is a double-edged responsibility. For there have been and are now today despotic or tyrannical forms of governments that have committed horrendous acts upon humanity. The subjects of these governments have not only a right but also a duty to violate policies of these governments that are contrary to the explicit will of the Bible. Those in authority have a responsibility to reward that which is good and have enough respect for the law to do justice to that which is evil. The governing power is a minister of God, and they need to be subject to the Lordship of Jesus and take the responsibility to rule for our good. If those who govern insist on violating that which is good, then be fearful of whatever punishment God will mete out. So those governing have a great responsibility, just as those being governed have the responsibility to be in subjection to the divine Master.

Paul was able to utilize the authority and principles of a dictatorial government (Acts 25:11; 27). He would appeal to that government on issues that were consistent with Scripture, in principle, to the advantage of the Gospel of Christ. He received transportation all the way to Rome at the cost of tax payers because he appealed his case to the Roman government. Christianity did not overthrow the mighty Roman Empire by force, but by love and implementing the moral standards of the New Testament into the hearts of even those in the household of Caesar (Phil. 4:22). Such is the power of the Gospel unto salvation. In our day, we might do well to impose this same set of standards.

Romans 13:4 says, "…for it is a minister of God to you for good. But if you do what is evil, be afraid; for it does not bear the sword for nothing; for it is a minister of God, an avenger who brings wrath on the one who practices evil." We need to appreciate that governing is a ministry of God. He can vent wrath upon those who practice evil, and this is only to be feared if we practice evil. If we do not practice evil, we should have no fear of being governed, assuming the government is in harmony with the principles that God has laid upon them.

Romans 13:5: "Therefore it is necessary to be in subjection, not only because of wrath, but also for conscience sake." Now this is kind of interesting. The conscience we have been given recognizes the need to be governed. We need to be subject to leadership. Our belief and our conscience are innately aware of the need. The government is to be sustained by the populace that it governs, thus we pay taxes. The payment of taxes is a Biblical principle. As verses 6–7 say, "For because of this you also pay taxes, for rulers are servants of God, devoting themselves to this very thing. Render to all what is due them: tax to whom tax is due; custom to whom custom; fear to whom fear; honor to whom honor." The rulers need to appreciate their ministry to God in their act of governing. When this concept is absent, the degree of fairness in governing and the practice of governing for the good of the people will be lost.

QUESTIONS AND DISCUSSION FOR OUR RELATIONSHIP TO THE PRINCIPLE OF GOVERNING

1. God establishes the principle of _____ (verse 1).

2. Do not _____ authority.

3. Who does the condemning?

4. A matter of behavior results in _____ or _____ (verses 3 and 4).

5. Name two reasons for subjection: _____ and _____ (See verse 5.)

6. What are the instructions about payment of taxes? (See verses 6 and 7.)

Subjection to the Greater Law

Romans 13:8–10

So in the first seven verses we see a dual responsibility of the governed and the governing, such that each is answerable to God. Each has a definite place within the ordinance of God. If both live within the will of God, then society will indeed be free, prosperous, and decent. Should one or both entities violate those principles, society suffers, and ultimately the ruling force weakens and subjects itself to overthrow.

In this next verse we have a little change of pace. We are shifting from talking about the broadness of governing to discussing more about the governing of ourself, our attitudes, and our actions towards one another. Romans 13:8 says, "Owe nothing to anyone except to love one another; for he who loves his neighbor has fulfilled the law." Taking this out of context, we could insert credit cards and all sorts of debts here. While this may be sound judgment, remember the context. This verse refers to our being governed and not necessarily to debt. There are other ways in which we can be indebted to our neighbors, and we should never place ourselves in a position where we are under an obligation to them other than to love them. The philosophy of "I'll scratch your back if you scratch mine" is causing our neighbors, and us, to perform tasks that are not out of love but out of obligation. You and your neighbor will get along much better if deeds performed are motivated by concern and love, with no expectations.

"Owe nothing to anyone except to love one another; for he who loves his neighbor has fulfilled the law." This verse really is super. We need to appreciate that our first debt is to love one another. In loving one another, we fulfill the law. In Matthew Chapter 5, Jesus teaches that He did not come to destroy the Law and the Prophets but that He came to fulfill the Law. In Romans we have this phrase "fulfilled the law" used again. While Jesus came to fulfill the Law, here we find that love fulfills the Law. Jesus was certainly the perfect and beautiful and complete example of love fulfilling the Law. The love He put forth to fulfill the Law has resulted in our being governed by the Holy Spirit rather than by the spirit of the flesh.

Next Paul goes back and reaches into the very teeth of the Law itself. Romans 13:9: "For this, *you shall not commit adultery, you shall not murder, you shall not steal, you shall not covet,* and if there is any other commandment, it is summed up in this saying, *you shall love your neighbor as yourself.*'" If you love your neighbor as you love yourself, sexual promiscuity, hatred, and envy will be counted as obsolete, for they will be swallowed up in our love for our neighbor. Verse 10: "Love does no wrong to a neighbor; therefore love is the fulfillment of the law." In John 13:34–35, Jesus raised this law a step higher. He said, "A new commandment I give to you, that you love one another, even as I have loved you, that you also love one another. By this all men will know that you are My disciples, if you have love for one another." We are to love one another as Jesus loved us. Jesus' love is totally sacrificial. This is the kind of love that fulfills the Law.

QUESTION AND DISCUSSION FOR SUBJECTION TO THE GREATER LAW

1. Discuss ways in which we can be in debt to our neighbors other than financially and in loving them.

2. We are to fulfill the _____ to our neighbor with _____ (verses 8–10).

3. Tell how Jesus' love fulfilled the Law.

Words of Exhortation

Romans 13:11–14

Romans 13:11: "Do this, knowing the time, that it is already the hour for you to awaken from sleep; for now salvation is nearer to us than when we believed." There are a lot of different schools of thought about the meaning of this verse, but I would like to look at just a couple of them. An interesting timeline can be associated with this verse. The timeline is justified in ticking here because of the phrase "…the hour for you to awaken from sleep…" Was it that the Roman church was asleep? Perhaps. This is often preached when preachers try to awaken a church to their responsibility. But there is a deeper and more interesting approach to be taken relative to the salvation we shall ultimately receive. We are now nearer than when we first believed to being forever with God in heaven and freed from the limitations of time and matter as we now experience them. This is a comparison that suggests what we do now is like sleepwalking compared to the full vision of God's warmth, grace, and blessings that we shall receive when we are with Him face to face. The encouragement here is for us to awaken from this sleep, realizing and having a great spiritual vision of something in addition to the glories of our salvation today that shall be ours in the days to come.

Romans 13:12: "The night is almost gone and the day is near." Each day is a day spent, and the night is closer at hand when our physical departure will be made. It is not to be counted as gloomy or gory, but it is to be counted as a day of great reward, of great victory, and of a full awaking of ourselves into the very presence of God. "Therefore let us lay aside the deeds of darkness and put on the armor of light." Here is an encouragement for us to lay aside the peanuts of things and grab for the pearls of personal relationships to really appreciate the best qualities of life. The best quality of life is to see our neighbors included in the family of God. Our greatest passion for our neighbors is that they may find the greatest relationship of all—a relationship with God. This can be seen in one of Jesus' final face to face encounters with his apostles prior to His ascension. They were told to go into all of the world and preach the Gospel, making disciples. If we do this for our neighbors, we shall surely see love for our neighbors being fully exhibited.

Romans 13:13–14: "Let us behave properly as in the day, not in carousing and drunkenness, not in sexual promiscuity and sensuality, not in strife and jealousy. But put on the Lord Jesus Christ…" What a difference there is in our daily lives since we have put on Jesus. The putting on of Jesus involves the putting on of His character, the adopting of the principles that He stands for, and the embracing of His teachings. The putting on of Jesus was initiated when we accepted Christ and when we were baptized. We read in Galatians 3:27, "For all of you who were baptized into Christ have clothed yourselves with Christ." Verse 14 continues, "…and make no provision for the flesh in regard to its lusts." We don't need to provide for the lusts of the flesh. We endured that involuntary servitude before we were joined with Christ (Romans 6:14). But now we are in a voluntary servitude to the Lord Jesus Christ, and with the help of the Holy Spirit, we do not need to be bound by the lusts of the flesh (Romans 8:3–11).

To recap this chapter, we find that we should be true to the principles of governing. There is an obligation attached to these principles that good should be rewarded and evil punished. We have a responsibility to ourselves and to our neighbors to love our neighbors as Christ loved us.

QUESTIONS AND DISCUSSION FOR WORDS OF EXHORTATION

1. Why a "wake-up" call? (See verse 11.)

2. What is the difference between day and night? (See verses 12–13.)

3. Name three or four things that are involved in the putting on of Jesus.

Chapter 14

RELATIONSHIPS WITH CHRISTIANS OF VARIOUS SPIRITUAL LEVELS
ROMANS 14:1–23

Introduction

IN THE PREVIOUS chapter we discussed that we have an obligation to love our neighbor even as we love ourselves. This is easily seen but sometimes not as easily executed. Chapter 14 will help us with the execution of this principle, regardless of whether we view ourselves as strong in the faith or as needing strength. Watch your toes, because we are going to do a little bit of stomping.

Accept the Weak in Faith

Romans 14:1–3

Romans 14:1-3: "Now accept the one who is weak in faith, but not for the purpose of passing judgment on his opinions." I want to consider the object of faith here as it develops in this chapter. Think it through with me, patiently. This faith is not faith toward God. Rather it is toward one another and faith toward, or belief in, opinions. Keeping that in mind, let us press on. Verse 2: "One person has faith that he may eat all things but he who is weak eats vegetables only." His faith is relative to what he can eat. One has faith that he can eat all things, and another man has faith that restricts his diet such that he eats only vegetables. This does not mean that that person has a weak faith in God, but instead he has a weak faith regarding the eating of meat. He might have weak faith from a dietary standpoint, from a cholesterol standpoint, or he may take it from the pages of the Old Testament in which certain meats were forbidden. Wherever that weakness is, the person has a weakness of faith regarding the eating of meat, not in regard to God. Verse 3: "The one who eats is not to regard with contempt the one who does not eat, and the one who does not eat is not to judge the one who eats, for God has accepted him." God accepts both the meat eater and the vegetarian. It is not a matter of faith in God; it is a matter of conscience towards things rather than towards God.

QESTIONS AND DISCUSSION FOR ACCEPT THE WEAK IN FAITH

1. What is the wrong reason for the strong to accept the weak? (See verses1–2.)

2. What is the "object" of faith? God or things? (See verse 2.)

3. Strong =_____ weak =_____ (verse 3).

The Matter of Judging

Romans 14:4–12

Romans 14:4: "Who are you to judge the servant of another?" What a great question! We do this a lot. We compare our hair dressers and lawn services. We are critical of coaches, teachers, and preachers. We know how to do it better, how it "should" look or be. We have our preferences, and of course, we are right. But in reality, we don't have a right to judge another man's servant. Verse 4 continues, "To his own master he stands or falls; and he will stand, for the Lord is able to make him stand." The master is the one who pays or hires the servant. Verse 5: "One person regards one day above another, another regards every day alike. Each person must be fully convinced in his own mind." When we are convinced in our own minds and act according to our consciences, we are not sinning, even if another does not hold that same conviction. Nor are others sinning, for this is a matter of conscience, not of a command of God. Verse 6: "He who observes the day, observes it for the Lord, and he who eats, does so for the Lord, for he gives thanks to God; and he who eats not, for the Lord he does not eat, and gives thanks to God." The bottom line is that it doesn't matter if a person is feasting or fasting on any particular day. If he or she is giving thanks to God, honoring God, and acting within his or her conscience, others shall not determine whether or not that person's behavior is acceptable to God. That is surely between the individual and God. So we must each focus on our own behavior regarding diet and relationships.

Romans 14:7–8: "For not one of us lives for himself, and not one dies for himself; for if we live, we live for the Lord, or if we die, we die for the Lord; therefore whether we live or die, we are the Lord's." The pearl is in serving the Lord. The days and the diet are the peanuts. Let's separate the peanuts from the pearls. We must appreciate that we live unto God and not allow a difference of conscience, procedure, or tradition to create disfellowship and/or disrespect for each other. In matters of doctrine we want unity, in matters of opinion, liberty, and in all things love.

Romans 14:9: "For to this end Christ died and lived again, that He might be Lord both of the dead and of the living." In other words, to the "end" that we live for Him or die for Him is the culmination of our faith. It is not seen in whether we live or whether we die but for the purpose of our life and death. This is our emulating the purpose for which Christ died. Verse 10: "But you, why do you judge your brother? Or you again, why do you regard your brother with contempt? For we will all stand before the judgment seat of God." Let us focus on the pearls of relationship with acceptance and toss the peanuts that disrupt. If we kept our eyes on what is important, Christendom would have a whole lot fewer divisions and schisms. We would be able to embrace others who have differences in the manner in which they serve God, even if their practices and traditions are not the same as ours. We would be able to embrace them as we ought as brethren in Christ.

Romans 14:11–12: "For it is written, 'AS I LIVE, SAYS THE LORD, EVERY KNEE SHALL BOW TO ME, AND EVERY TONGUE SHALL GIVE PRAISE TO GOD.' So, then, each one of us will give an account of himself to God." No one is exempt. Everyone must give an account to God according to the integrity and honesty he or she has developed with his or her own conscience. Each answers to God and not man.

QUESTIONS AND DISCUSSION FOR THE MATTER OF JUDGING

1. The weak are not to _____ the _____ another. (See verse 4.)

2. What two illustrations are used _____ and _____ (verses 5–6).

3. We both do what we do as unto the _____ (verses 7–8).

4. Christ _____ and _____ for _____ (verse 9).

5. The strong and weak will both stand before the _____ of God (verses 10–11).

6. We are accountable for _____ (verse12).

An Alternative to Judging is Removing Obstacles in the Way of Others

Romans 14:13–23

Romans 14:13: "Therefore let us not judge one another anymore, but rather determine this—not to put an obstacle or a stumbling block in a brother's way." If you invite somebody over to dinner and you know that person is a vegetarian, you don't serve up roast beef or a ham sandwich. You respect the person's decision even though you don't share it. Verse 14: "I know and am convinced in the Lord Jesus that nothing is unclean in itself…" It is in the manner or means in which it is used that it becomes unclean. Now, in my particular physical condition, to eat a whole slew of French fries would endanger my health. I should consider doing so as unclean, but a person who is not physically vulnerable to fatty cholesterol could eat French fries. I should not look down upon him or her with distain. Verse 14 continues, "…but to him who thinks anything to be unclean, to him it is unclean." To illustrate—I think habitually eating food of high cholesterol count is unclean, but that does not necessarily mean it is unclean to everyone. To me it is, and I need to exercise the restraint because I know how harmful it would be to me. This has a great application to our dietary intent. Consequently, a great deal of this chapter is spent upon the subject of food.

Romans 14:15: "For if because of food your brother is hurt, you are no longer walking according to love. Do not destroy with your food him for whom Christ died." In other words, don't use your peanuts to destroy a pearl. We can get a lot more mileage from this concept than just dietary things. How many problems do we have in the church today because we elevate the peanuts of opinion above the pearls of relationships with our brothers and sisters? We want the preacher to attract people to the church, and yet, we chase them away faster than they can be brought in. We squabble over peanuts and toss away the pearls that have been brought to Christ. Each one of us needs to consider seriously, with a great deal of thought and prayer, what we hold as essential and what we hold as nonessential. The basis for this determination should be in what the Bible expressly denounces or acclaims as matters that are essential. Matters that are not specifically articulated in the Scriptures but are held to by different segments of "churchanity" are void of our passing judgment.

Romans 14:16–17: "Therefore do not let what is for you a good thing be spoken of as evil; for the kingdom of God is not eating and drinking, but righteousness and peace and joy in the Holy Spirit." These verses offer the best definition of that which constitutes the kingdom of God here on earth. It is not about eating and drinking, it is in righteousness, peace, joy, and the Holy Spirit. Our entry into the kingdom of God is not determined so much by what we do as by who we are. Are we a person at peace with ourself and at peace with God? Are we a person with great joy in our life and great joy before the Lord, desiring only to be led of the Holy Spirit? If you answered yes to these questions, then you are a person who will do what the witness of the Holy Spirit has given you through the Scriptures. For Scripture is the voice of the Holy Spirit. This is a rung higher than many of us have reached; but reach for it, stretch for it, grab it, and climb it—that is the challenge of this chapter.

Romans 14:18–19 (parentheses mine): "For he who in this way serves Christ is acceptable to God and approved by men. So then we pursue (chase, follow after, throwing aside things that hinder our pursuit) the things which make for peace and the building up of one another." This is really the application of the Golden Rule, loving your neighbor as yourself, and further, not living just for ourselves but living for Christ and benefiting those who are in Christ. Verse 20: "Do not tear down the work of God for the sake of food." For the peanuts of this world—things that—even if you feel as though they are allowable, if you use them in an offensive way they become evil. Verse 21: "It is good not to eat meat or to drink wine, or to do anything by which your brother stumbles." If you like to eat meat or if you like a glass of wine and you know it is going to cause somebody to stumble, do it at home, not in public. Do it in private; don't gloat over it or flaunt it. Even when we are acting within our own consciences we must be sensitive not to create a stumbling block for somebody for whom Jesus died.

Romans 14:22: "The faith which you have…" (that is, the faith in things, not relating to the faith in God, rather the faith in what you can or can't do) "…have as your own conviction before God. Happy is he who does not condemn himself in what he approves." In other words, if you approve of something, you can allow yourself to act accordingly, with a clear conscience. But if you doubt something and violate that, you are going to be one miserable person. You must either change your convictions or quit practicing the behavior that violates your conscience. Verse 23: "But he who doubts is condemned if he eats, because his eating is not from faith; and whatever is not from faith is sin." This statement is probably the most misused phrase, especially within many brotherhoods. Keep "whatever is not from faith is sin" in the intended context. It is not referring to faith in God, but to faith in things.

QUESTIONS AND DISCUSSION FOR AN ALTERNATIVE TO JUDGING IS REMOVING OBSTACLES IN THE WAY OF OTHERS

1. Don't _____ nor cause another to stumble (verse 13).

2. In the Lord, what of itself is unclean? Is there an exception? (See verse 14.)

3. Christ died for both the _____ and _____ (verse 15).

4. What three things constitute God's kingdom? (See verses 16–19.)

5. How can we make unclean out of that which is clean? (See verses 20–21.)

6. How can we jeopardize our faith and happiness? (See verses 22–23.)

7. Key verses to this chapter are 14 and 17. Do you agree? If not, why? If so, why?

Chapter 15

CONCLUDING REMARKS AND WORDS OF ENCOURAGEMENT
ROMANS 15:1–33

Introduction

WE NOW TURN to the fifteenth chapter, which in part is really a continuation of the fourteenth chapter. We should consider it not as a beginning of a new thought, but rather as further discussion of our obligations toward those who we consider weak or those who we consider strong or those who hold a difference of opinion. We should try not to be a stumbling block in front of them.

Jesus, Our Example for Helping the Weak

Romans 15:1–7

Romans 15:1: "Now we who are strong ought to bear the weaknesses of those without strength and not just please ourselves." What a difference of emphasis here. In the last chapter we saw what we should *not* do in placing stumbling blocks and in judging. Now in the fifteenth chapter, we find the attitude we *should* have and the actions that we *ought* to take. We are commanded to bear one another's weaknesses. To further understand "to bear the weaknesses," let's review Romans 14:1, which says, "Now accept the one who is weak in faith, but not for the purpose of passing judgment on his opinions." So, rather than being judgmental towards others, we are to be accommodating towards them, and we can help to bear their weaknesses.

Romans 15:2: "Let each of us please his neighbor for his good, to his edification." This means pleasing our neighbor, even those with an opinion different than ours. Verse 3: "For even Christ did not please Himself; but as it is written, *'the reproaches of those who reproached you fell on me.'*" If we are to have the mind of Christ in us, that is, if we are to emulate the actions of

Jesus, we are to follow in His steps. Peter so eloquently wrote in 1 Peter 2:21, "For you have been called for this purpose, since Christ also suffered for you, leaving you an example for you to follow in His steps." We need to adopt as a part of our makeup, as a part of our character, a good relationship with our neighbors who are of a different persuasion than we are. Isolation is not a formula for success.

Romans 15:4: "For whatever was written in earlier times was written for our instruction, so that through perseverance and the encouragement of the Scriptures we might have hope." This refers to many verses in the Old Testament. Note Psalm 69:9. "For zeal for your house has consumed me." It is when we are totally immersed in His grace, in His word, can the hope in our heart be pass on to the world.

Romans 15:5: "Now may the God who gives perseverance and encouragement grant you to be of the same mind with one another according to Christ Jesus…" This type of exhortation is repeated in Philippians 2:5, where it says, "Have this attitude in yourselves which was also in Christ Jesus…"

Romans 15:6–7: "…so that with one accord you may with one voice glorify the God and Father of our Lord Jesus Christ. Therefore, accept one another, just as Christ also accepted us to the glory of God." Jesus took us where we were and as we were. This is where we need to be in our acceptance of other people. Sure, they may not be where God wants them to be, but neither are we where God would like for us to be. God has not rejected us or judged us or condemned us or belittled us. He has accepted us. Why, then, can't we, with that same attitude, go forth and work with other people. They may not do things the same way we would do them or have the same convictions about all the things we do. Nonetheless, they are the Lord's, and we need to accept them as such.

QUESTIONS AND DISCUSSION FOR
JESUS, OUR EXAMPLE FOR HELPING THE WEAK

1. Strong to bear the weakness of _____. Why? (See verse 1.)

2. Give two reasons why we are to please our neighbor (verse 2).

3. How did Christ set the example? (See verses 3–4.)

4. How might we have hope? 1. _____ 2. _____ 3. _____ (See verse 4.)

5. What is the key of these scriptures? (Note Philippians 2:5–11.)

6. Note the benefits of these qualities (verse 6).

7. Note the purpose of these qualities (verse 7).

Christ the Servant to both Jews and Gentiles

Romans 15:8–13

Romans 15:8–9: "For I say that Christ has become a servant to the circumcision on behalf of the truth of God to confirm the promises given to the fathers, and for the Gentiles to glorify God for His mercy…" Next we find a large quotation from various passages of Scripture—one from Deuteronomy, another from Psalms, and another from Isaiah. These all reflect upon the inclusion of the Gentiles into the family of God and how that has brought great joy and great hope to the Gentiles. It is in this hope that Paul concludes after these passages from the Old Testament. Verses 9–13 read, "…as it is written, *'therefore I will give praise to you among the gentiles, and I will sing to your name.'* Again he says, *'rejoice, o gentiles, with his people.'* And again, *'praise the lord all you gentiles, and let all the peoples praise him.'* Again Isaiah says, *'there shall come the root of jesse, and he who arises to rule over the gentiles, in him shall the gentiles hope.'* Now may the God of hope fill you with all joy and peace in believing, so that you will abound in hope by the power of the Holy Spirit." Paul shares his earnest hope for both Jews and Gentiles that they will be filled with hope for all instead of just for themselves, filled with all joy rather than animosity for others of different backgrounds, and filled with peace. This is beyond human accomplishment, and so we must rely upon the power of the Holy Spirit to do this and to grant us a heart of inclusion.

QUESTIONS AND DISCUSSION FOR
CHRIST THE SERVANT TO BOTH JEWS AND GENTILES

1. Why did Christ become a _____ to the Jews? (See verse 8.)

2. Why did Christ become a _____ to the Gentiles? (See verse 9.)

3. Christ became a servant to the Gentiles to _____ God and to show His _____ (verses 9–12; Ps. 18:49; Deut. 32:43; Ps. 117:7; Isa. 11:10).

4. What is the theme of the Old Testament verses quoted in verses 10–12?

5. List the attributes with which we are to be filled (verse 13).

6. Name some of the fruits of the Holy Spirit seen in verse 13 (see Gal. 5:22–23).

Paul's Regard for the Christians at Rome

Romans 15:14–33

Romans 15:14–16: "And concerning you, my brethren, I myself also am convinced that you yourselves are full of goodness, filled with all knowledge and able also to admonish one another. But I have written very boldly to you on some points so as to remind you again, because of the grace that was given me from God, to be a minister of Christ Jesus to the Gentiles, ministering as a priest the gospel of God, so that my offering of the Gentiles may become acceptable, sanctified by the Holy Spirit." Paul is sharing here with the people where he has come from, what his ministry is, and how he has poured himself out. He poured himself out for those who he could have so easily judged because of their differences of understanding and culture. Instead of judging them, he went to them and brought them the great peace of God.

Romans 15:17: "Therefore in Christ Jesus I have found reason for boasting in things pertaining to God." That should be our only posture of boasting. It is in Christ. We should not consider ourselves as anything special except as what God has made special of us through Christ. Verse 18: "For I will not presume to speak of anything except what Christ has accomplished through me, resulting in the obedience of the Gentiles by word and deed…" So Paul here is completely excusing himself from any ego or from any perseverance upon his own will. He is giving all of that glory and honor to the Lord Jesus Christ. Verse 19: "…in the power of signs and wonders, in the power of the Spirit; so that from Jerusalem and round about as far as Illyricum I have fully preached the gospel of Christ." What a missionary! His missionary spirit brought him to a position to where he was able to say that he had preached the full Gospel and had fully preached that Gospel to those in Jerusalem and as far as Illyricum, which was one of the stops on his first missionary journey.

Romans 15:20–23: "And thus I aspired to preach the gospel, not where Christ was already named, so that I would not build on another man's foundation; but as it is written '*they who had no news of him shall see, and they who have not heard shall understand.*' For this reason I have often been prevented from coming to you but now, with no further place for me in these regions, and since I have had for many years a longing to come to you…" He wants to preach where no one else has preached, and though he has a longing to come to them, it will be just a passing through kind of a venture. Verses 24–25: "…whenever I go to Spain—for I hope to see you in passing, and to be helped on my way there by you, when I have first enjoyed your company for a while—but now, I am going to Jerusalem serving the saints." He was planning on seeing them, though those plans were somewhat derailed for awhile. Paul was heading back toward Jerusalem, there to be imprisoned. Even though he was heading back to Jerusalem, it was his longing to go onto Spain and that passing through on his way to Spain for which he would need their help. As we will see in the later verses, he here is asking for financial or material assistance.

Romans 15:26: "For Macedonia and Achaia have been pleased to make a contribution for the poor among the saints in Jerusalem." The churches in Macedonia and Achaia have already helped him. Verse 27: "Yes, they were pleased to do so, and they are indebted to them. For if the Gentiles have shared in their spiritual things, they are indebted to minister to them also in material things." So here is a principle that those who proclaim the Gospel are worthy of having their material needs met by those who have received spiritual blessings from them. This principle should not be abused by those who are preaching the Gospel or be neglected by those who are the recipients of the Gospel. Verses 28–29: "Therefore, when I have finished this, and have put my seal on this fruit of theirs, I will go on by way of you to Spain. I know that when I come to you, I will come in the fullness of the blessing of Christ."

In verse 30, Paul begins his final thoughts on this particular area of self denial, the preaching of Christ, and urging people to pray for him. In principle Paul goes back to Romans 12:1, where he urged them to present their bodies as living sacrifices. He now states another beseeching or urging in Romans 15:30: "Now I urge you, brethren, by our Lord Jesus Christ and by the love of the Spirit, to strive together with me in your prayers to God for me…" What a beautiful verse, where a man is sharing his feelings and longing, yearning for the prayers from others in his service to Christ. Paul is pouring out his heart to them in his service, and he is now asking them to pour out their hearts to God in prayer for him. Verses 31–32: "…that I may be rescued from those who are disobedient in Judea, and that my service for Jerusalem may prove acceptable to the saints; so that I may come to you in joy by the will of God and find refreshing rest in your company." A prayer that he might be delivered from those in Jerusalem and Judea, a prayer that he might come to them in the joy and will of God and find rest with them is now what he needs.

The servant of God who brings the Gospel and the recipients of that Gospel minister each to the other. The joy of bringing shown by the servant and the refreshing encouragement and rest shown by the recipient are evident so that both may savor the peace of God. "Now the God of peace be with you all. Amen" (verse 33).

QUESTIONS AND DISCUSSION FOR
PAUL'S REGARD FOR THE CHRISTIANS AT ROME

1. What are the complements Paul pays to the saints in Rome? (See verses 14–21.)

2. What is the main reason for Paul not having been in Rome? (See verses 22–29.) And what is the indication as to when the book of Romans was written? (Note Acts 20:1–6; 21:1–14.)

3. What are the words of encouragement? (See verses 30–33.)

4. What are the benefits of prayer to both Paul and the saints at Rome? (See verses 30–33.)

GREETINGS, WARNINGS, AND BENEDICTION
ROMANS 16:1–27

Introduction

THIS CHAPTER IS one that presents us with a number of unique things. It helps us to understand the size of the group there at Rome. It was a large group of Christians. Whether they met as one body or in various congregations, we don't know, but there were many people. We do know of one congregation, and that was in Prisca and Aquila's home. From this we could infer that there were other congregations. There were many who had worked with Paul before. There were many whom Paul had personally brought to the Lord Jesus Christ. There were many who had worked for Christ that Paul knew of only by reputation. Paul goes through a whole list of people and extends his greetings. This is always a dangerous thing to do, because you are liable to leave somebody out.

Paul must have had such a terrific mind and such a deep personal relationship with people—the type that we don't usually sense and see. We appreciate his theology. We appreciate his relationship with the Lord. We appreciate his deep understanding of God's grace. Here we see a little bit of an insight into the heart of Paul as far as his public and personal relations are concerned. Sometimes he is criticized for having poor manners or poor public relations. One example of this is the dispute that he had with Barnabas about John Mark on the first missionary journey (Acts 15:36–38). Other examples include the bluntness that he used with people in his letters, and even with the apostle Peter (Gal. 2:11–21). But here in the sixteenth chapter, as you read through the greetings that he gives to people, you see the heart that he has for people and how people have responded in their great love for him. In reality he was a very tender man and a man who was considerate and conscious about the welfare of others. He wants them to know of his concern for them and wants to be sure that they appreciate his love for them. So as you browse through these greetings, keep this in mind.

Commendation and Greetings

Romans 16:1–16

Romans 16:1–15: "I commend to you our sister Phoebe, who is a servant of the church which is at Cenchrea; that you receive her in the Lord in a manner worthy of the saints, and that you help her in whatever matter she may have need of you; for she herself has also been a helper of many, and of myself as well. Greet Prisca and Aquila, my fellow workers in Christ Jesus, who for my life risked their own necks, to whom not only do I give thanks, but also all the churches of the Gentiles; also greet the church that is in their house. Greet Epaenetus, my beloved, who is the first convert to Christ from Asia. Greet Mary, who has worked hard for you. Greet Andronicus and Junias, my kinsmen and my fellow prisoners, who are outstanding among the apostles, who also were in Christ before me. Greet Ampliatus, my beloved in the Lord. Greet Urbanus, our fellow worker in Christ, and Stachys my beloved. Greet Apelles, the approved in Christ. Greet those who are of the household of Aristobulus. Greet Herodion, my kinsman. Greet those of the household of Narcissus, who are in the Lord. Greet Tryphaena and Tryphosa, workers in the Lord. Greet Persis the beloved, who has worked hard in the Lord. Greet Rufus, a choice man in the Lord, also his mother and mine. Greet Asyncritus, Phlegon, Hermes, Patrobas, Hermas and the brethren with them. Greet Philologus and Julia, Nereus and his sister, and Olympas, and all the saints who are with them."

In verse 16, after he has gone through the majority of those whom he wishes to greet and wishes to extend his love and warmth and remembrance of bygone days to, he says, "Greet one another with a holy kiss. All the churches of Christ greet you." In this phrase "the churches of Christ," note that the word "church" is not capitalized and that it is not singular. I don't know of a place in the Scriptures where "church of Christ" is used in a singular sense. As far as I have seen, this term is used in the generic sense in greetings as assemblies or congregations or fellowships of Christ. I think that needs to be noted. Neither is the term "Christian church" mentioned within the Scriptures. The term "Christian," however, is mentioned three times (Acts 11:26, in reference to disciples; Acts 26:28, in reference to an individual; 1 Peter 4:16, in reference to a vast number of individuals in various locations). Generally speaking, these terms are the same. In the name "church of Christ," "Christ" is a possessive pronoun referring back to church. This indicates that the church belongs to Christ. In the term "Christian church," the word "Christian" is Christ with a possessive suffix added to it, which denotes that the Christian church belongs to Christ.

Sometimes we get tied up in terminology and squabble over these terms that cause divisions within the fellowship of Christ's church. We even question at times the redemption of others due to human application of biblical terminology. How we need to grow and get beyond these things, realizing that when we have accepted Him, we are in God's church and involved in His love. When we become obedient to Him in accordance with the dictates of the Scriptures, He has added us to His church. It is His church, and only He does the adding. We need to be very careful about doing the subtracting, for all we are doing is subtracting from a man-created, local congregation, which may not be at all in accordance with the mathematics of God.

QUESTIONS AND DISCUSSION FOR COMMENDATION AND GREETINGS

1. Phoebe may have been the bearer of the letter. Would this explain the special treatment Paul wanted to be shown to her? (See verse 1.)

2. Why should Phoebe be received and cared for? (See verse 2.)

3. Why should special notice be given to Prisca and Aquila? (See verses 3–5.)

4. What do the greetings to twenty-seven of the Christians in Rome demonstrate of Paul's knowledge and concern for the congregations in Rome? (See verses 3–16.)

Final Warning and Word of Encouragement

Romans 16:17–20

Romans 16:17–19:"Now I urge you, brethren, keep your eye on those who cause dissensions and hindrances contrary to the teaching which you learned, and turn away from them. For such men are slaves, not of our Lord Christ but of their own appetites; and by their smooth and flattering speech they deceive the hearts of the unsuspecting. For the report of your obedience has reached to all; therefore I am rejoicing over you, but I want you to be wise in what is good and innocent in what is evil." Boy, isn't that something? Be wise in what is good and innocent in evil (or in not having knowledge of evil). Verse 20: "The God of peace will soon crush Satan under your feet…" There are three theories as to the fulfillment of this prophetic statement. That Satan will be crushed under your feet could refer to:

- The freedom from Satan's bondage and hence his being crushed out of your life (Romans 6 and 7).

- That Satan is referred to here as the Roman Empire and that the power of the Gospel would soon be Rome's demise (Romans 1:18–32).
- The complete absence of Satan in heaven that we shall experience when we reach our ultimate goal (Revelation 21 and 22).

This is a beautiful little doxology or closing thought as he comes to the conclusion of this verse (20), "…the grace of our Lord Jesus be with you."

QUESTIONS AND DISCUSSION FOR COMMENDATION AND GREETINGS

1. Why the warning to those who would not surrender as servants of Christ? (See verses 17–18.)

2. What is the cause for rejoicing, and when is ignorance good? (See verse 19.)

3. The prophetic statement: "The God of peace will soon crush Satan under your feet…" may refer to what three things? (See verse 20.)

Commendation and Greetings (continued)

Romans 16:21–24

Now Paul adds a P.S. He has a few little comments to make regarding those who are with him and their wishes to express their greetings to those in Rome as he also has done. Romans 16:21–23: "Timothy my fellow worker greets you, and so do Lucius and Jason and Sosipater, my kinsmen. I, Tertius, who write this letter, greet you in the Lord. Gaius, host to me and to the whole church, greets you, Erastus, the city treasurer greets you, and Quartus, the brother." The city treasurer is interesting, because he was the treasurer of the city of Corinth. I have seen his name carved in stone that once stood over the archway to the treasury house at Corinth. Verse 24: "[The grace of our Lord Jesus Christ be with you all. Amen.]"

QUESTION AND DISCUSSION FOR
COMMENDATION AND GREETINGS (CONTINUED)

1. Notice the greetings from those who are traveling with Paul. What does this show of Paul's character? (See verses 21–23. Note Acts 19:21–22.)

Benediction

Romans 16:25–27

In Romans 16:25–27, Paul concludes this fantastic, fabulous doctrinal book and includes the practical applications we saw in the last five chapters: "Now to Him who is able to establish you according to my gospel and the preaching of Jesus Christ, according to the revelation of the mystery which has been kept secret for long ages past, but now is manifested, and by the Scriptures of the prophets, according to the commandment of the eternal God, has been made known to all the nations, leading to obedience of faith; to the only wise God, through Jesus Christ, be the glory forever. Amen."

In these last three verses Paul sums up the entirety of faith. Paul restates the very heartbeat of this book of Romans. He sums Romans up by returning us to that first chapter of the good news of the Gospel and the preaching of the Gospel. It is this power of God unto salvation through the revealing of righteousness and through the revealing of that mystery. That mystery of righteousness was fully enacted by the coming of Jesus Christ. The mystery revealed is no longer now a mystery, but one that is fully known. It was manifested by prophecy through the Old Testament Scriptures. It was manifested in accordance with the commands and directions of the eternal God. Now the Gospel is being made known to all the nations, just as Jesus in His Great Commission desired and commanded. It is the Gospel that gives us instructions as to how to live obedient in faith. The book of Romans ends with the wisdom of God that is seen through the beauty of Jesus Christ and through the means of our access to this grace by faith.

Bless the Lord, oh my soul!

QUESTIONS AND DISCUSSION FOR BENEDICTION

1. Name the qualities of the Gospel mentioned in the benediction (verses 25–27).

2. Name the qualities of Jesus mentioned in the benediction (verses 25–27).

3. Name the qualities of God mentioned in the benediction (verses 25–27).

4. How long will these qualities last?

OUTLINE OF THE BOOK OF ROMANS

Chapter 1: The Gospel—the Theme—Romans 1:1–17
    Introduction to the Letter—Romans 1:1–2
    Introduction of Paul and the Gospel—Romans1:1–2
    Introduction of Jesus, the Good News of God—Romans 1:3–7
    Giving Thanks to God—Romans 1:8–17

Chapter 2: All-Inclusive Need—Romans 1:18–3:20
    Introduction
    Power to Overcome the Sins of the Gentiles—Romans 1:18–32
    Power to Overcome the Sins of the Jews—Romans 2:1–2:29
    Addressing Objections—Romans 3:1–20

Chapter 3: Christ's Righteousness Plus Man's Faith Gains Salvation—Romans 3:21–31
    Introduction
    Righteousness and Faith—Romans 3:21–22
    The Need, the Remedy—Romans 3:23–31

Chapter 4: Faith as Man's Reaction to God's Action of Redemption—Romans 4:1–25
    Introduction
    Justification and Works—Romans 4:1–8
    Justification and Faith—Romans 4:9–12
    The Test of Faith—Romans 4:13–25

Breinigsville, PA USA
26 November 2010

250045BV00005B/97-146/P